U0898294

本书出版得到《大中华文库》出版经费资助

大中华文库

LIBRARY

OF CHINESE CLASSICS

大中华文库

汉英对照

LIBRARY OF CHINESE CLASSICS

Chinese-English

三字经　千字文　孝经

THE THREE-CHARACTER CANON
THE THOUSAND CHARACTER WRITING
THE BOOK OF FILIAL PIETY

[宋] 王应麟　著

Written by Wang Yinglin

孟凡君　译注

Translated by Meng Fanjun

[梁] 周兴嗣　著

Written by Zhou Xingsi

彭发胜　译注

Translated by Peng Fasheng

顾丹柯　译注

Translated by Gu Danke

First Edition 2015

ISBN 978-7-5001-4230-0

Published by
China Translation & Publishing House
Floor 6 Wuhua Building, 4(A) Chegongzhuang Street, Xicheng District
Beijing 100044, China
http: // www.ctph.com.cn
Printed by
Jiaxinda Printing Co., Shenzhen, China
Printed in the People's Republic of China

总　　序

杨牧之

《大中华文库》终于出版了。我们为之高兴，为之鼓舞，但也倍感压力。

当此之际，我们愿将郁积在我们心底的话，向读者倾诉。

一

中华民族有着悠久的历史和灿烂的文化，系统、准确地将中华民族的文化经典翻译成外文，编辑出版，介绍给全世界，是几代中国人的愿望。早在几十年前，西方一位学者翻译《红楼梦》，将书名译成《一个红楼上的梦》，将林黛玉译为“黑色的玉”。我们一方面对外国学者将中国的名著介绍到世界上去表示由衷的感谢，一方面为祖国的名著还不被完全认识，甚而受到曲解，而感到深深的遗憾。还有西方学者翻译《金瓶梅》，专门摘选其中自然主义描述最为突出的篇章加以译介。一时间，西方学者好像发现了奇迹，掀起了《金瓶梅》热，说中国是“性开放的源头”，公开地在报刊上鼓吹中国要“发扬开放之传统”。还有许多资深、友善的汉学家译介中国古代的哲学著作，在把中华民族文化介绍给全世界的工作方面作出了重大贡献，但或囿于理解有误，或缘于对中国文字认识的局限，质量上乘的并不多，常常是隔靴搔痒，说不到点子上。大哲学家黑格尔曾经说过：中国有最完备的国史。但他认为中国古代没有真正意义上的哲学，还处在哲学史前状态。这么了不起的哲学家竟然作出这样大失水准的评论，何其不幸。正如任何哲学家都要受时间、地点、条件的制约一样，黑格尔也离不开这一规律。当时他也只能从上述水平的汉学家译过去的文字去分析、理解，所以，黑格尔先生对中国古代社会的认识水平是什么状态，也就不难想象了。

中国离不开世界，世界也缺少不了中国。中国文化摄取外域的新成分，丰富了自己，又以自己的新成就输送给别人，贡献于世界。从公元5世纪开始到公元15世纪，大约有一千年，中国走在世界的前列。在这一千多年的时间里，她的光辉照耀全世界。人类要前进，怎么能不全面认识中国，怎么能不认真研究中国的历史呢？

二

中华民族是伟大的，曾经辉煌过，蓝天、白云、阳光灿烂，和平而兴旺；也有过黑暗的、想起来就让人战栗的日子，但中华民族从来是充满理想，不断追求，不断学习，渴望和平与友谊的。

中国古代伟大的思想家孔子曾经说过："三人行，必有我师焉。择其善者而从之，其不善者而改之。"孔子的话就是要人们向别人学习。这段话正是概括了整个中华民族与人交往的原则。人与人之间交往如此，在与周边的国家交往中也是如此。

秦始皇第一个统一了中国，可惜在位只有十几年，来不及做更多的事情。汉朝继秦而继续强大，便开始走出去，了解自己周边的世界。公元前138年，汉武帝派张骞出使西域。他带着一万头牛羊，总值一万万钱的金帛货物，作为礼物，开始西行，最远到过“安息”（即波斯）。公元73年，班超又率36人出使西域。36个人按今天的话说，也只有一个排，显然是为了拜访未曾见过面的邻居，是去交朋友。到了西域，班超派遣甘英作为使者继续西行，往更远处的大秦国（即罗马）去访问，“乃抵条支而历安息，临西海以望大秦”（《后汉书·西域传》）。“条支”在“安息”以西，即今天的伊拉克、叙利亚一带，“西海”应是今天的地中海。也就是说甘英已经到达地中海边上，与罗马帝国隔海相望，“临大海欲渡”，却被人劝阻而未成行，这在历史上留下了遗恨。可以想见班超、甘英沟通友谊的无比勇气和强烈愿望。接下来是唐代的玄奘，历经千难万险，到“西天”印度取经，带回了南亚国家的古老文化。归国后，他把带回的佛教经典组织人翻译，到后来很多经典印度失传了，但中国却保存完好，以至于今天，没有玄奘的《大唐西域记》，印度人很难编写印度古代史。明代郑和“七下西洋”，把中华文化传到东南亚一带。鸦片战争以后，一代又一代先进的中国人，为了振兴中华，又前赴后继，向西方国家学习先进的科学思想和文明成果。这中间有我们的领导人朱德、周恩来、邓小平；有许许多多大科学家、文学家、艺术家，如郭沫若、李四光、钱学森、冼星海、徐悲鸿等。他们的追求、奋斗，他们的博大胸怀、兼收并蓄的精神，为人类社会增添了光彩。

中国文化的形成和发展过程，就是一个以众为师、以各国人民为师，不断学习和创造的过程。中华民族曾经向周边国家和民族学习过许多东西，假如没有这些学习，中华民族绝不可能创造出昔日的辉煌。回顾历史，我们怎么能够不对伟大的古埃及文明、古希腊文明、古印度文明满怀深深的感激？怎么能够不对伟大的欧洲文明、非洲文明、美洲文明、澳洲文明，以及中国周围的亚洲文明充满温情与敬意？

中华民族为人类社会曾作出过独特的贡献。在15世纪以前，中国的科学技术一直处于世界遥遥领先的地位。英国科学家李约瑟说："中国在公元3世纪到13世纪之间，保持着一个西方所望尘莫及的科学知识水平。"美国耶鲁大学教授、《大国的兴衰》的作者保罗·肯尼迪坦言："在近代以前时期的所有文明中，没有一个国家的文明比中国更发达，更先进。"

世界各国的有识之士千里迢迢来中国观光、学习。在这个过程中，中国唐朝的长安城渐渐发展成为国际大都市。西方的波斯、东罗马，东亚的高丽、新罗、百济、南天竺、北天竺，频繁前来。外国的王侯、留学生，在长安供职的外国官员，商贾、乐工和舞士，总有几十个国家，几万人之多。日本派出"遣唐使"更是一批接一批。传为美谈的日本人阿倍仲麻吕（晁衡）在长安留学的故事，很能说明外国人与中国的交往。晁衡学成仕于唐朝，前后历时五十余年。晁衡与中国的知识分子结下了深厚的友情。他归国时，传说在海中遇难身亡。大诗人李白作诗哭悼："日本晁卿辞帝都，征帆一片远蓬壶。明月不归沉碧海，白云愁色满苍梧。"晁衡遇险是误传，但由此可见中外学者之间在中国长安交往的情谊。

后来，不断有外国人到中国来探寻秘密，所见所闻，常常让他们目瞪口呆。《希腊纪事》（希腊人波桑尼阿著）记载公元2世纪时，希腊人在中国的见闻。书中写道："赛里斯人用小米和青芦喂一种类似蜘蛛的昆虫，喂到第五年，虫肚子胀裂开，便从里面取出丝来。"从这段对中国古代养蚕技术的描述，可见当时欧洲人与中国人的差距。公元9世纪中叶，阿拉伯人来到中国。一位阿拉伯作家在他所著的《中国印度闻见录》中记载了曾旅居中国的阿拉伯商人的见闻：

——一天，一个外商去拜见驻守广州的中国官吏。会见时，外商总盯着官吏的胸部，官吏很奇怪，便问："你好像总盯着我的胸，这是怎么回事？"那位外商回答说："透过你穿的丝绸衣服，我隐约看到你胸口上长着一个黑痣，这是什么丝绸，我感到十分惊奇。"官吏听后，失声大笑，伸出胳膊，说："请你数数吧，看我穿了几件衣服？"那商人数过，竟然穿了五件之多，黑痣正是透过这五层丝绸衣服显现出来的。外商惊得目瞪口呆，官吏说："我穿的丝绸还不算是最好的，总督穿的要更精美。"

——书中关于茶（他们叫干草叶子）的记载，可见阿拉伯国家当时还没有喝茶的习惯。书中记述："中国国王本人的收入主要靠盐税和泡开水喝的一种干草税。在各个城市里，这种干草叶售价都很高，中国人称这种草叶叫'茶'，这种干草叶比苜蓿的叶子还多，也略比它香，稍有苦味，用开水冲喝，治百病。"

——他们对中国的医疗条件十分羡慕，书中记载道："中国人医疗条件很好，穷人可以从国库中得到药费。"还说："城市里，很多地方立一石碑，高10肘，上面刻有各种疾病和药物，写明某种病用某种药医治。"

——关于当时中国的京城，书中作了生动的描述：中国的京城很大，人口众多，一条宽阔的长街把全城分为两半，大街右边的东区，住着皇帝、宰相、禁军及皇家的总管、奴婢。在这个区域，沿街开凿了小河，流水潺潺；路旁，葱茏的树木整然有序，一幢幢宅邸鳞次栉比。大街左边的西区，住着庶民和商人。这里有货栈和商店，每当清晨，人们可以看到，皇室的总管、宫廷的仆役，或骑马或步行，到这里来采购。

此后的史籍对西人来华的记载，渐渐多了起来。13世纪意大利旅行家马可·波罗，尽管有人对他是否真的到过中国持怀疑态度，但他留下一部记述元代事件的《马可·波罗游记》却是确凿无疑的。这部游记中的一些关于当时中国的描述使得西方人认为是“天方夜谭”。总之，从中西文化交流史来说，这以前的时期还是一个想象和臆测的时代，相互之间充满了好奇与幻想。

从16世纪末开始，由于航海技术的发展，东西方航路的开通，随着一批批传教士来华，中国与西方开始了直接的交流。沟通中西的使命在意大利传教士利玛窦那里有了充分的体现。利玛窦于1582年来华，1610年病逝于北京，在华二十余年。除了传教以外，做了两件具有历史象征意义的事，一是1594年前后在韶州用拉丁文翻译《四书》，并作了注释；二是与明代学者徐光启合作，用中文翻译了《几何原本》。

西方传教士对《四书》等中国经典的粗略翻译，以及杜赫德的《中华帝国志》等书对中国的介绍，在西方读者的眼前展现了一个异域文明，在当时及稍后一段时期引起了一场“中国热”，许多西方大思想家的眼光都曾注目于中国文化。有的推崇中华文明，如莱布尼兹、伏尔泰、魁奈等，有的对中华文明持批评态度，如孟德斯鸠、黑格尔等。莱布尼兹认识到中国文化的某些思想与他的观念相近，如周易的卦象与他发明的二进制相契合，对中国文化给予了热情的礼赞；黑格尔则从他整个哲学体系的推演出发，认为中国没有真正意义上的哲学，还处在哲学史前的状态。但是，不论是推崇还是批评，是吸纳还是排斥，中西文化的交流产生了巨大的影响。随着先进的中国科学技术的西传，特别是中国的造纸、火药、印刷术和指南针四大发明的问世，大大改变了世界的面貌。马克思说："中国的火药把骑士阶层炸得粉碎，指南针打开了世界市场并建立了殖民地，而印刷术则变成了新教的工具，变成对精神发展创造必要前提的最强大的杠杆。"英国的哲学家培根说：中国的四大发明"改变了全世界的面貌和一切事物的状态"。

三

大千世界，潮起潮落。云散云聚，万象更新。中国古代产生了无数伟大的科学家：祖冲之、李时珍、孙思邈、张衡、沈括、毕昇……产生了无数科技成果：《齐民要术》、《九章算术》、《伤寒杂病论》、《本草纲目》……以及保存至今的世界奇迹：浑天仪、地动仪、都江堰、敦煌石窟、大运河、万里长城……但从15世纪下半叶起，风水似乎从东方转到了西方，落后的欧洲只经过400年便成为世界瞩目的文明中心。英国的牛顿、波兰的哥白尼、德国的伦琴、法国的居里、德国的爱因斯坦、意大利的伽利略、俄国的门捷列夫、美国的费米和爱迪生……光芒四射，令人敬仰。

中华民族开始思考了。潮起潮落究竟是什么原因？中国人发明的火药，传到欧洲，转眼之间反成为欧洲列强轰击中国大门的炮弹，又是因为什么？

鸦片战争终于催醒了中国人沉睡的迷梦，最先"睁眼看世界"的一代精英林则徐、魏源迈出了威武雄壮的一步。曾国藩、李鸿章搞起了洋务运动。中国的知识分子喊出"民主与科学”的口号。中国是落后了，中国的志士仁人在苦苦探索。但落后中饱含着变革的动力，探索中孕育着崛起的希望。“向科学进军”，中华民族终于又迎来了科学的春天。

今天，世界毕竟来到了21世纪的门槛。分散隔绝的世界，逐渐变成联系为一体的世界。现在，全球一体化趋势日益明显，人类历史也就在愈来愈大的程度上成为全世界的历史。当今，任何一种文化的发展都离不开对其他优秀文化的汲取，都以其他优秀文化的发展为前提。在近现代，西方文化汲取中国文化，不仅是中国文化的传播，更是西方文化自身的创新和发展；正如中国文化对西方文化的汲取一样，既是西方文化在中国的传播，同时也是中国文化在近代的转型和发展。地球上所有的人类文化，都是我们共同的宝贵遗产。既然我们生活的各个大陆，在地球史上曾经是连成一气的“泛大陆”，或者说是一个完整的“地球村”，那么，我们同样可以在这个以知识和学习为特征的网络时代，走上相互学习、共同发展的大路，建设和开拓我们人类崭新的“地球村”。

西学仍在东渐，中学也将西传。各国人民的优秀文化正日益迅速地为中国文化所汲取，而无论西方和东方，也都需要从中国文化中汲取养分。正是基于这一认识，我们组织出版汉英对照版《大中华文库》，全面系统地翻译介绍中国传统文化典籍。我们试图通过《大中华文库》，向全世界展示，中华民族五千年的追求、五千年的梦想，正在新的历史时期重放光芒。中国人民就像火后的凤凰，万众一心，迎接新世纪文明的太阳。

1999年8月　北京

FOREWORD TO THE *LIBRARY OF CHINESE CLASSICS*

Yang Muzhi

The publication of the *Library of Chinese Classics* is a matter of great satisfaction to all of us who have been involved in the production of this monumental work. At the same time, we feel a weighty sense of responsibility, and take this opportunity to explain to our readers the motivation for undertaking this cross-century task.

1

The Chinese nation has a long history and a glorious culture, and it has been the aspiration of several generations of Chinese scholars to translate, edit and publish the whole corpus of the Chinese literary classics so that the nation's greatest cultural achievements can be introduced to people all over the world. There have been many translations of the Chinese classics done by foreign scholars. A few dozen years ago, a Western scholar translated the title of *A Dream of Red Mansions* into "A Dream of Red Chambers" and Lin Daiyu, the heroine in the novel, into "Black Jade." But while their endeavours have been laudable, the results of their labours have been less than satisfactory. Lack of knowledge of Chinese culture and an inadequate grasp of the Chinese written language have led the translators into many errors. As a consequence, not only are Chinese classical writings widely misunderstood in the rest of the world, in some cases their content has actually been distorted. At one time, there was a "*Jin Ping Mei* craze" among Western scholars, who thought that they had uncovered a miraculous phenomenon, and published theories claiming that China was the "fountainhead of eroticism," and that a Chinese "tradition of permissiveness" was about to be laid bare. This distorted view came about due to the translators of the *Jin Ping Mei (Phan in the Golden Vase)* putting one-sided stress on the raw elements in that novel, to the neglect of its overall literary value. Meanwhile, there have been many distinguished and well-intentioned Sinologists who have attempted to make the culture of the Chinese nation more widely known by translating works of ancient Chinese philosophy. However, the quality of such work, in many cases, is unsatisfactory, often missing the point entirely. The great philosopher Hegel considered that ancient China had no philosophy in the real sense of the word, being stuck in philosophical "prehistory." For such an eminent authority to make such a colossal error of judgment is truly regrettable. But, of course, Hegel was just as subject to the constraints of time, space and other objective conditions as anyone else, and since he had to rely for his knowledge of Chinese philosophy on inadequate translations it is not difficult to imagine why he went so far off the mark.

China cannot be separated from the rest of the world; and the rest of the world cannot ignore China. Throughout its history, Chinese civilization has enriched itself by absorbing new elements from the outside world, and in turn has contributed to the progress of world civilization as a whole by transmitting to other peoples its own cultural achievements. From the 5th to the 15th centuries, China marched in the front ranks of world civilization. If mankind wishes to advance, how can it afford to ignore China? How can it afford not to make a thoroughgoing study of its history?

2

Despite the ups and downs in their fortunes, the Chinese people have always been idealistic, and have never ceased to forge ahead and learn from others, eager to strengthen ties of peace and friendship.

The great ancient Chinese philosopher Confucius once said, "Wherever three persons come together, one of them will surely be able to teach me something. I will pick out his good points and emulate them; his bad points I will reform." Confucius meant by this that we should always be ready to learn from others. This maxim encapsulates the principle the Chinese people have always followed in their dealings with other peoples, not only on an individual basis but also at the level of state-to-state relations.

After generations of internecine strife, China was unified by Emperor

Qin Shi Huang (the First Emperor of the Qin Dynasty) in 221 BC The Han Dynasty, which succeeded that of the short-lived Qin, waxed powerful, and for the first time brought China into contact with the outside world. In 138 BC, Emperor Wu dispatched Zhang Qian to the western regions, i.e. Central Asia. Zhang, who traveled as far as what is now Iran, took with him as presents for the rulers he visited on the way 10,000 head of sheep and cattle, as well as gold and silks worth a fabulous amount. In 73 AD, Ban Chao headed a 36-man legation to the western regions. These were missions of friendship to visit neighbours the Chinese people had never met before and to learn from them. Ban Chao sent Gan Ying to explore further toward the west. According to the "Western Regions Section" in the *History of Later Han*, Gan Ying traveled across the territories of present-day Iraq and Syria, and reached the Mediterranean Sea, an expedition which brought him within the confines of the Roman Empire. Later, during the Tang Dynasty, the monk Xuan Zang made a journey fraught with danger to reach India and seek the knowledge of that land. Upon his return, he organized a team of scholars to translate the Buddhist scriptures, which he had brought back with him. As a result, many of these scriptural classics which were later lost in India have been preserved in China. In fact, it would have been difficult for the people of India to reconstruct their own ancient history if it had not been for Xuan Zang's *A Record of a Journey to the West in the Time of the Great Tang Dynasty*. In the Ming Dynasty, Zheng He transmitted Chinese culture to Southeast Asia during his seven voyages. Following the Opium Wars in the mid-19th century, progressive Chinese, generation after generation, went to study the advanced scientific thought and cultural achievements of the Western countries. Their aim was to revive the fortunes of their own country. Among them were people who were later to become leaders of China, including Zhu De, Zhou Enlai and Deng Xiaoping In addition, there were people who were to become leading scientists, literary figures and artists, such as Guo Moruo, Li Siguang, Qian Xuesen, Xian Xinghai and Xu Beihong. Their spirit of ambition, their struggles and their breadth of vision were an inspiration not only to the Chinese people but to people all over the world.

Indeed, it is true that if the Chinese people had not learned many things from the surrounding countries they would never have been able to produce the splendid achievements of former days. When we look back upon history, how can we not feel profoundly grateful for the legacies of the civilizations of ancient Egypt, Greece and India? How can we not feel fondness and respect for the cultures of Europe, Africa, America and Oceania?

The Chinese nation, in turn, has made unique contributions to the community of mankind. Prior to the 15th century, China led the world in science and technology. The British scientist Joseph Needham once said, "From the third century AD to the 13th century AD China was far ahead of the West in the level of its scientific knowledge." Paul Kennedy, of Yale University in the U.S., author of *The Rise and Fall of the Great Powers*, said, "Of all the civilizations of the pre-modern period, none was as well-developed or as progressive as that of China."

Foreigners who came to China were often astonished at what they saw and heard. The Greek geographer Pausanias in the second century AD gave the first account in the West of the technique of silk production in China: "The Chinese feed a spider-like insect with millet and reeds. After five years the insect's stomach splits open, and silk is extracted therefrom." From this extract, we can see that the Europeans at that time did not know the art of silk manufacture. In the middle of the 9th century AD, an Arabian writer includes the following anecdote in his *Account of China and India*:

"One day, an Arabian merchant called upon the military governor of Guangzhou. Throughout the meeting, the visitor could not keep his eyes off the governor's chest. Noticing this, the latter asked the Arab merchant what he was staring at. The merchant replied, 'Through the silk robe you are wearing, I can faintly see a black mole on your chest. Your robe must be made out of very fine silk indeed!' The governor burst out laughing, and holding out his sleeve invited the merchant to count how many garments he was wearing. The merchant did so, and discovered that the governor was actually wearing five silk robes, one on top of the other, and they were made of such fine material that a tiny mole could be seen through them all! Moreover, the governor explained that the robes he was wearing were not made of the finest silk at all; silk of the highest grade was reserved for the garments worn by the provincial governor."

The references to tea in this book (the author calls it "dried grass") reveal that the custom of drinking tea was unknown in the Arab countries at that time: "The king of China's revenue comes mainly from taxes on salt and the dry leaves of a kind of grass which is drunk after boiled water is poured on it. This dried grass is sold at a high price in every city in the country. The Chinese call it 'cha.' The bush is like alfalfa, except that it bears more leaves, which are also more fragrant than alfalfa. It has a slightly bitter taste, and when it is infused in boiling water it is said to have medicinal properties."

Foreign visitors showed especial admiration for Chinese medicine. One wrote, "China has very good medical conditions. Poor people are given money to buy medicines by the government."

In this period, when Chinese culture was in full bloom, scholars flocked from all over the world to China for sightseeing and for study. Chang'an, the capital of the Tang Dynasty was host to visitors from as far away as the Byzantine Empire, not to mention the neighboring countries of Asia. Chang'an, at that time the world's greatest metropolis, was packed with thousands of foreign dignitaries, students, diplomats, merchants, artisans and entertainers. Japan especially sent contingent after contingent of envoys to the Tang court. Worthy of note are the accounts of life in Chang'an written by Abeno Nakamaro, a Japanese scholar who studied in China and had close friendships with ministers of the Tang court and many Chinese scholars in a period of over 50 years. The description throws light on the exchanges between Chinese and foreigners in this period. When Abeno was supposedly lost at sea on his way back home, the leading poet of the time, Li Bai, wrote a eulogy for him.

The following centuries saw a steady increase in the accounts of China written by Western visitors. The Italian Marco Polo described conditions in China during the Yuan Dynasty in his *Travels*. However, until advances in the science of navigation led to the opening of east-west shipping routes at the beginning of the 16th century Sino-Western cultural exchanges were coloured by fantasy and conjecture. Concrete progress was made when a contingent of religious missionaries, men well versed in Western science and technology, made their way to China, ushering in an era of direct contacts between China and the West. The experience of this era was embodied in the career of the Italian Jesuit Matteo Ricci. Arriving in China in 1582, Ricci died in Beijing in 1610. Apart from his missionary work, Ricci accomplished two historically symbolic tasks — one was the translation into Latin of the "Four Books," together with annotations, in 1594; the other was the translation into Chinese of Euclid's *Elements*.

The rough translations of the "Four Books" and other Chinese classical works by Western missionaries, and the publication of Père du Halde's *Description Geographique, Historique, Chronologique, Politique, et Physique de l'Empire de la Chine* revealed an exotic culture to Western readers, and sparked a "China fever," during which the eyes of many Western intellectuals were fixed on China. Some of these intellectuals, including Leibniz, held China in high esteem; others, such as Hegel, nursed a critical attitude toward Chinese culture. Leibniz considered that some aspects of Chinese thought were close to his own views, such as the philosophy of the *Book of Changes* and his own binary system. Hegel, on the other hand, as mentioned above, considered that China had developed no proper philosophy of its own. Nevertheless, no matter whether the reaction was one of admiration, criticism, acceptance or rejection, Sino-Western exchanges were of great significance. The transmission of advanced Chinese science and technology to the West, especially the Chinese inventions of paper-making, gunpowder, printing and the compass, greatly changed the face of the whole world. Karl Marx said, "Chinese gunpowder blew the feudal class of knights to smithereens; the compass opened up world markets and built colonies; and printing became an implement of Protestantism and the most powerful lever and necessary precondition for intellectual development and creation." The English philosopher Roger Bacon said that China's four great inventions had "changed the face of the whole world and the state of affairs of everything."

3

Ancient China gave birth to a large number of eminent scientists, such as Zu Chongzhi, Li Shizhen, Sun Simiao, Zhang Heng, Shen Kuo and Bi Sheng. They produced numerous treatises on scientific subjects, including *The Manual of Important Arts for the People's Welfare, Nine Chapters on the Art of Mathematics, Treatise on Febrile Caused by Cold* and *Compendium of Materia Medica*. Their accomplishments included ones whose influence has been felt right down to modern times, such as the armillary sphere, seismograph, Dujiangyan water conservancy project, Dunhuang Grottoes, Grand Canal and Great Wall. But from the latter part of the 15th century, and for the next 400 years, Europe gradually became the cultural centre upon which the world's eyes were fixed. The world's most outstanding scientists then were England's Isaac Newton, Poland's Copernicus, France's Marie Curie, Germany's Rontgen and Einstein, Italy's Galileo, Russia's Mendelev and America's Edison.

The Chinese people then began to think: What is the cause of the rise and fall of nations? Moreover, how did it happen that gunpowder, invented in China and transmitted to the West, in no time at all made Europe powerful enough to batter down the gates of China herself?

It took the Opium War to wake China from its reverie. The first generation to make the bold step of "turning our eyes once again to the rest of the world" was represented by Lin Zexu and Wei Yuan. Zeng Guofan and Li Hongzhang started the Westernization Movement, and later intellectuals raised the slogan of "Democracy and Science." Noble-minded patriots, realizing that China had fallen behind in the race for modernization, set out on a painful quest. But in backwardness lay the motivation for change, and the quest produced the embryo of a towering hope, and the Chinese people finally gathered under a banner proclaiming a "March Toward Science."

On the threshold of the 21st century, the world is moving in the direction of becoming an integrated entity. This trend is becoming clearer by the day. In fact, the history of the various peoples of the world is also becoming the history of mankind as a whole. Today, it is impossible for any nation's culture to develop without absorbing the excellent aspects of the cultures of other peoples. When Western culture absorbs aspects of Chinese culture, this is not just because it has come into contact with Chinese culture, but also because of the active creativity and development of Western culture itself; and vice versa. The various cultures of the world's peoples are a precious heritage which we all share. Mankind no longer lives on different continents, but on one big continent, or in a "global village." And so, in this era characterized by an all-encompassing network of knowledge and information we should learn from each other and march in step along the highway of development to construct a brand-new "global village."

Western learning is still being transmitted to the East, and vice versa. China is accelerating its pace of absorption of the best parts of the cultures of other countries, and there is no doubt that both the West and the East need the nourishment of Chinese culture. Based on this recognition, we have edited and published the *Library of Chinese Classics* in a Chinese-English format as an introduction to the corpus of traditional Chinese culture in a comprehensive and systematic translation. Through this collection, our aim is to reveal to the world the aspirations and dreams of the Chinese people over the past 5,000 years and the splendour of the new historical era in China. Like a phoenix rising from the ashes, the Chinese people in unison are welcoming the cultural sunrise of the new century.

August 1999 Beijing

目　录

三字经 1

千字文 103

孝经 233

CONTENTS

The Three-Character Canon 1

The Thousand Character Writing 103

The Book of Filial Piety 233

大中华文库

汉英对照

LIBRARY OF CHINESE CLASSICS

Chinese-English

三字经

THE THREE-CHARACTER CANON

[宋] 王应麟　著

Written by Wang Yinglin

孟凡君　译注

Translated by Meng Fanjun

《三字经》简述

《三字经》堪称是在中国广为流传、影响深远的蒙学著作，其作者一般认为是南宋硕儒王应麟（1223—1296）。但实际上早在王应麟之前，《三字经》的雏形就已出现，如宋人项安世曾道："古人教童子多用韵语，如……《三字训》之类。"（《项氏家说》）项安世早生于王应麟一百多年，故《三字训》可看作是《三字经》的前身。不管怎样，鉴于早期的《三字经》叙述历代兴灭尽至宋代，故可断定《三字经》的最早成稿年代应在宋元时期。因此，说《三字经》的作者为宋人王应麟，料无大谬。

《三字经》问世之后即风靡华夏，成为宋代以后中国广为采用的蒙学读本，可以说，时至今日，未读过《三字经》的汉家蒙童恐怕寥寥无几。随着《三字经》影响的日渐扩大，对《三字经》的注释和增益也不断出现，特别是明清以来，不仅《三字经》的注释本、注音本、绘图本日渐增多，而且其内容也随着朝代的更替而不断增益，产生出各种不同的增补本，其中流传最广的，应推清道光年间贺兴思编纂的《三字经注解备要》，故笔者选用的《三字经》原文，就是贺兴思的注解备要本。

随着《三字经》影响的日益扩大，对《三字经》的翻译也开始逐步展开。早在清朝前期，为了便于《三字经》在满蒙等族中流传，《三字经》开始被译成满文和蒙文，其中以陶格敬译的《满文三字经》和菘岩富俊译的《蒙汉三字经》影响较大。另外，至清末时期，《三字经》也开始被译成外国文字，逐渐流传海外，其中影响较大者，有卫方济的拉丁译本，儒莲的法译本，和裨志文、翟理斯和艾泰尔的英译本。以上译本固然出自西洋人士之手，其语文表达固然无可指摘，但该译者的非汉语文化语境，自然使他们对华夏传统文化的真谛缺乏足够的了解，故对《三字经》所蕴含的文化精髓的把握不免会带有因文化隔阂而产生的某些偏颇。鉴于此，在当今中西文化全面交汇的时代大势下，站在华夏文化语境的角度对《三字经》进行更为准确的解读与传译，是一项既必要又极有意义的任务。

《三字经》之所以一经问世便流传不衰，其要有二：一、具有朗朗上口的韵律美感；二、具有言简意赅的教化功用。而在《三字经》的翻译中，这两大特征同样不容忽视。从理论角度而言，翻译《三字经》，既应传达出原文的韵律美感，也应传达出原文的教化功用，这样方能尽善尽美。而从翻译实践的角度而言，在跨文化语境的语言转换中，这种试图尽善尽美的译事目标却极难达到，因为，欲传达《三字经》原文的韵律美，自然以韵文译之为佳，但若斤斤于韵脚之穿凿，实有因声伤意之虞，美则美矣，难于尽善；而欲再现其言意间的教化功用，自然以达意传实为上，但若亟亟于言意之究竟，恐又有以意害韵之嫌，善则善矣，却难于尽美。善美难以两全之际，译者往往不得已而求其次，或彰其美声而损益其辞，或显其实意而放任其韵。

质言之，译事之妙，唯在二心：自心，他心。自心即经营译事之勇猛精进心，他心即体贴读者之方便分别心。二心合一，译事之至也。

About *The Three-Character Canon*

The Three-Character Canon can be considered the most popular and influential enlightening work in China. The author is generally considered to be Wang Yinglin (1223–1296), a learned scholar in the Southern Song Dynasty. As a matter of fact, however, the embryonic form of *The Three-Character Canon* had emerged before Wang Yinglin published it. For instance, Xiang Anshi, a historical figure of the Song Dynasty, once said, "The ancient people tended to enlighten their children with rhyming words, such as *The Three-Character Admonition,* etc." (*Family Precept of Xiang*). Xiang Anshi lived more than a hundred years earlier than Wang Yinglin; *The Three-Character Admonition,* therefore, can be regarded as the predecessor of *The Three-Character Canon*. Anyhow, seeing that the historical account ends with the Song Dynasty in its early editions, we know for sure that the earliest edition of *The Three-Character Canon* must have been published in the period between the Song and the Yuan dynasties. Thus, it is plausible to determine that the author of *The Three-Character Canon* was Wang Yinglin.

The Three-Character Canon is popular all over China, having been immediately adopted following the Song Dynasty as a textbook for children. To this date, so to speak, few Chinese children have failed to read *The Three-Character Canon*. With its gradually expanding influence, a great amount of work has been done to annotate and augment it. Since the Ming and Qing dynasties, in particular, *The Three-Character Canon* has improved not only in form, but also in content. Various editions of *The Three-Character Canon,* such as the annotated, the phonetic and the illustrated editions, etc. have appeared. On the other hand, it has also been expanded upon in content with the alternation of dynasties, bringing about various revised editions, the most popular being *The Annotated Edition of The Three-Character Canon* compiled by He Xingsi, a scholar during the reign of Emperor Daoguang in the Qing Dynasty. *The Three-Character Canon* chosen as the original in this book is the very edition compiled by He Xingsi.

With the enlarged influence of *The Three-Character Canon*, steps were taken to translate it. In the early stages of the Qing Dynasty, for example, translations began for the Manchu and Mongolian languages to make it convenient to be learned by those ethnic groups. Of these, the most influential was the Manchu translated by Tao Gejing, and the Mongolian by Songyan Fujun. And what's more, during the late Qing, translations had begun in foreign languages, such as into Latin by Francais Noël, into French, by Julien, and the English versions, by Bridgman, Gilles and Yitaier. These have exerted larger influences than other versions. Though they were translated by foreigners who were sound in the expression of their own languages, yet it is probable that being unawere of the Chinese cultural context would prevent them from thoroughly absorbing the true spirit of the traditional Chinese, which would have more or less misled them in the exact interpretation of the work's cultural spirit. Hence, it is of great necessity and significance for us to interpret and translate *The Three-Character Canon* now, more exactly in the cultural context of China today, that exists alongside a greater level of exchange between Chinese and western cultures.

The reason why *The Three-Character Canon* has exerted such a continual lasting influence lies in its two features, namely its rhyming beauty, which makes it quite readable, and its instructiveness, which is conveyed in its conciseness. Theoretically, a translation of *The Three-Character Canon* should convey not only the original rhyming beauty, but also the original instructiveness, by means of which a perfect version could be obtained. Practically, however, it's extremely difficult to make a perfect cross-cultural context version, because to convey its original rhyming beauty, the translator needs to translate it in the verse form. If the translator tries to copy the original rhyming form without caring about the meaning it may result in a beautiful, but unfaithful version. On the contrary, if the translator emphasizes the instructiveness of the original without caring about faithfully conveying the original rhyming form, the rhyming beauty will be sacrificed for the original meaning. If the translator fails to acheive a perfect version with original beauty and faithful meaning united in harmony, the content will be second best, either being prior to its beautiful original rhyming forms by increasing or decreasing its original wording, or being prior to its original meaning leaving alone its original rhyming patterns. This publication adopts the form of an essay so as to enable the readers to get a thorough and exact understanding of the original meaning of *The Three-Character Canon*.

Essentially, the mystery of translation lies in two "hearts", namely, the heart of the "One", and the heart of the "Other". The former refers to the translator's desperate intention to obtain an exact version, and the latter, to the translator's delicate consideration of the variety of the version readers. The combination of the two "hearts" will bring about the most appropriate translation.

人之初，性本善。

性相近，习相远。

苟不教，性乃迁。

教之道，贵以专。

At the beginning of life,

Man is good-natured.

Human nature is alike,

Habits make them different.

For lack of education,

Nature is in alteration;

And the nurture of the young,

Better be maintained for long.

昔孟母，择邻处。

子不学，断机杼。

窦燕山，有义方。

教五子，名俱扬。

Once Mencius's mother
Chose the best neighborhood for her son;*
When her son played truant,
She cut the threads on the loom.†
Another case is Dou Yanshan,
Who was wise in family education.
He raised his five sons,
And all of them were blessed with fame.‡

* Mencius (孟子，372–289 B.C.), a great thinker during the Warring States Period. According to historical records, Mencius was very young when his father died. In order to raise him in sound surroundings, his mother Zhang（仉）moved home three times. Originally they lived near a graveyard, where she found her son imitating the acts of mourning. She thought it was bad for her son's upbringing, so she moved home to the town and they lived near a butcher's. There, however, she found her son imitating the acts of killing pigs and sheep. It was not a proper environment for her son, either. At last, the mother and son moved again and lived near a school, where young Mencius began to imitate the scholars' behavior and study. The mother was very pleased with this, and she decided to settle down there. This is the famous story of "Three Moves by Mencius' Mother".

† One day, seeing young Mencius run back home playing truant, his mother, who was weaving at the loom, became so angry that she cut all the threads on the loom off. She said to her son, "I'm weaving inch by inch, and if I cut off the threads now, I can no longer weave a piece of cloth. Your learning is the same as weaving cloth. If you fail to accumulate your knowledge day by day, you'll never succeed." Young Mencius was deeply sorry for his deed, and began to make great efforts in his studies, so much so, that he became a great thinker as well as a sage, second only to Confucius.

‡ Dou Yanshan（窦燕山）, a famous historical figure in the period of the Five Dynasties. His real name was Dou Yujun（窦禹钧）. Since he lived at the foot of Yanshan Mountain, he was also called Dou Yanshan. He had five sons, whom he raised in such a wise way that all of them became high government officials. This is the well-known story of "Five Sons, All Ascend".

养不教，父之过。

教不严，师之惰。

子不学，非所宜。

幼不学，老何为？

Rear children without instructing them,
And the father should be blamed;
Teach in a slack and lazy way
And the teacher should be criticized.
If a pupil plays truant,
It proves to be improper.
If a child fails to learn,
What could he be when old?

玉不琢，不成器。

人不学，不知义。

为人子，方少时。

亲师友，习礼仪。

Without being carved and polished,
Jade can't be a work of art.
If one does not learn,
He'll not know human virtues.
When one is young,
He should make the best of his time,
Associating with the good and the wise,
And learning to stand on ceremony.

香九龄，能温席。

孝于亲，所当执。

融四岁，能让梨。

弟于长，宜先知。

When Huang Xiang* was nine years old,
He would warm the mat for his father.
Whoever has love for their parents
Should be as kind as such.
When Kong Rong† was four years old,
He could offer his brothers the bigger pears.
Even if one is quite young,
One should love one's brothers.

* Huang Xiang (黄香), a historical figure during the period of the Eastern Han Dynasty. His mother died when he was young. He loved his father so much that during the hot summers he fanned his father to keep him cool, and during the cold winter he kept him warm. When he grew up, learned and noble, he became a minister in the government.

† Kong Rong (孔融，153–208), a high official and a man of letters in the late Han Dynasty, was one of the twentieth-generation disciples (followers) of Confucius.

首孝悌，次见闻。

知某数，识某文。

一而十，十而百。

百而千，千而万。

One should bear familial love from the outset
Before he starts to learn,
Including counting and computing,
As well as reading and writing.
One times ten is ten,
Ten times ten is a hundred,
A hundred times ten is a thousand,
And a thousand times ten is ten thousand.

三才者，天地人。

三光者，日月星。

三纲者，君臣义；

父子亲，夫妇顺。

There're three essential elements to know,

They are heaven, earth and man.

There are three kinds of light;

They're from the sun, the moon, and the stars.

There are three ethical disciplines:*

That of loyalty between the king and his men,

Of love between father and son,

And of harmony between husband and wife.

* The Three Ethical Disciplines are the basic rules of behavior in ancient China. According to the doctrines of the Confucianism of the Song School, the emperor should set the disciplines for his subjects（君为臣纲）; the father should set the disciplines for his sons（父为子纲）; and the husband should set the disciplines for his wife（夫为妻纲）. This is referred to as the Three Disciplines.

曰春夏，曰秋冬。

此四时，运不穷。

曰南北，曰西东。

此四方，应乎中。

There are Spring and Summer,
And Autumn and Winter:
They are the four seasons,
Alternating all the year round.
There is north and south,
And east and west:
They are the four directions,
Laid out from a central position.

曰水火，木金土。

此五行，本乎数。

曰仁义，礼智信。

此五常，不容紊。

There is water and fire,

Wood, metal, and earth:

They are five elements,

Related to the numerals.

There is benevolence, righteousness,

Courtesy, intelligence and loyalty.

They are the five human norms,

Which are regulated in certain terms.

稻粱菽，麦黍稷。

此六谷，人所食。

马牛羊，鸡犬豕。

此六畜，人所饲。

There is rice, sorghum and bean,
Wheat, millet and corn:
They are six kinds of grain
For one to serve as food,
There are the horse, the ox and the sheep,
The foul, the dog, and the pig:
They're six kinds of livestock,
Raised in herds by the farmers.

曰喜怒，曰哀惧；

爱恶欲，七情具。

匏土革，木石金；

丝与竹，乃八音。

There is joy and anger,

Sorrow and fear,

And is love, hate and desire:

They are seven human feelings altogether.

There are gourds, pottery, leather,

Wood, stone, and metal,

Together with string and bamboo,

All these can be made into musical instruments.

高曾祖，父而身；

身而子，子而孙；

自子孙，至玄曾。

乃九族，人之伦。

From his great-great-grandfather,
To his great-grandfather,
To his grandfather and father,
To himself and his son,
To his grandson and great-grandson,
And to his great–great-grandson:
Whoever is born into the world
Will face the nine-layer relation.*

* According to the ethical doctrines in ancient China, a person usually has nine-layer relations in the family, namely, 1) great-great-grandfather; 2) great-grandfather; 3) grandfather; 4) father; 5) self; 6) son; 7) grandson; 8) great-grandson; 9) great-great-grandson.

父子恩，夫妇从；

兄则友，弟则恭；

长幼序，友与朋；

君则敬，臣则忠。

There should be affection between father and son,

As well as love between husband and wife.

Brothers should be kind to each other:

The elder amiable, and the younger respectful.

A harmony should be maintained

Among families as well as friends.

Even the king should be cordial,

To whom the subjects will then be loyal.

此十义，人所同。

凡训蒙，须讲究。

详训诂，明句读。

为学者，必有初。

These are called the Ten Doctrines
That everyone in the world should follow.
To enlighten the school children,
Good methods must be taken.
The meaning must be correctly grasped,
And the syntax clear in mind.
A pupil must start his learning
From the very beginning.

小学终，至四书。

论语者，二十篇。

群弟子，记善言。

孟子者，七篇止。

After he has learned the basics,

He'd learn the Four Books* next.

The first book is *The Analects of Confucius*.

Composed of twenty chapters.

Which were recorded by his disciples

And put together as living doctrines.

The second book is called *The Mencius*,

Consisting of seven sections.

* The Four Books are the four basic Confucian classic works: *The Analects of Confucius* (*Lun Yu*), *The Mencius* (*Meng Zi*), *The Doctrine of the Mean* (*Zhong Yong*), *The Great Learning* (*Da Xue*).

讲道德，说仁义。

作中庸，子思笔。

中不偏，庸不易。

作大学，乃曾子。

In which is highlighted moralities,

As well as benevolence and righteousness.

The third book is *The Doctrine of the Mean*,

Written by Zi Si[*], Confucius' grandson.

Meets in the middle,

In which the common truth exists.

Zeng Zi[†] wrote *The Great Learning*,

From which one can achieve a great deal.

* Zi Si（子思，483–402 B.C.）, grandson of Confucius, and also called Kong Ji（孔伋）.

† Zeng Zi, the courtesy title of Zeng Shen（曾参，505–436 B.C.）, one of Confucius' disciples.

自修齐，至平治。

孝经通，四书熟。

如六经，始可读。

诗书易，礼春秋。

He demonstrated a way to self-improvement

From an individual life to social affairs.

When one's mastered *The Book of Filial Piety*,

Together with the four books,

The Six Confucian Scriptures*

Can be for him a new start.

The Songs, The Documents, and The Changes,

And *The Annals* and *The Rites*:

* The Six Confucian Scriptures are the basic readings of the Confucian School, namely, *The Book of Changes* (*Yi Jing*), *The Book of Songs* (*Shi Jing*), *The Book of Documents* (*Shu Jing* or *Shang Shu*), *The Book of Rites* (*Li Ji*), *The Book of Music* (*Yue Ji*), and *The Book of Annals* (*Chun Qiu* or *Spring and Autumn*).

号六经，当讲求。

有连山，有归藏；

有周易，三易详。

有典谟，有训诰；

Are called the Six Confucian Scriptures,
Which are needed to be studied thoroughly.
There was *Lianshan* in the Xia Dynasty,
Which was called *Guizang* in the Shang,
And *Zhouyi* in the Zhou,
All refer to *The Book of Changes*.
With the records of the early sages' deeds,
And with the regulations and laws.

有誓命，书之奥。

我周公，作周礼。

著六官，存治体。

大小戴，注礼记。

As well as the decrees and rules
The Book of Documents is hard to read.
A sage is called the Duke of Zhou,
Who drafted the rituals for the country.
He appointed six ministers*,
By whom the nation was governed.
Dai and his nephew† were two scholars,
Who annotated *The Book of Rites*.

* According to the records of *The Book of Rites*, the power of the government was shared by six ministers, namely, the Minister of Heaven (*Zhong Zai*), the Minister of Earth (*Si Tu*), the Minister of Spring (*Zong Bo*), the Minister of Summer (*Si Ma*), the Minister of Autumn (*Si Kou*), and the Minister of Winter (*Si Kong*). This is the embryonic form of the Six-Ministry System in ancient China.

† Dai was a famous scholar of the Han Dynasty. His full name was Dai De（戴德）. His nephew, whose name was Dai Sheng（戴圣）, was also a famous scholar. According to history, Dai De was called Senior Dai, and Dai Sheng, Junior Dai.

述圣言，礼乐备。

曰国风，曰雅颂。

号四诗，当讽咏。

诗既亡，春秋作。

By digging from the sage's words,

The *Book of Music* came from *The Rites*.

With *The National Morals*,

And *The Grace* and *The Paeans*.

The Book of Songs is divided into four sections,

And each should be chanted and recited.

When tradition of collecting folk songs is lost,

The Book of Annals was compiled.

寓褒贬，别善恶。

三传者，有公羊；

有左氏，有谷梁。

经既明，方读子。

Which sets the moral code for state officials,
And which judges the good from the evil.
Three commentaries have been given
To *The Book of Annals* ever written:
There are three commentary authors:
Gong Yang, Zuo Qiuming and Gu Liang.
After having grasped the classics,
One can read the works of other schools.

撮其要，记其事。

五子者，有荀扬；

文中子，及老庄。

经子通，读诸史。

Not only drawing up the essentials,

But also learning by heart the details.

Five figures should be mentioned

Of the great masters of thought:

They are named Xun Zi and Yang Zi,*

And Wen Zhong Zi, Lao Zi and Zhuang Zi.†

With a thorough understanding of the above mentioned,

* Xun Zi（荀子）, the honorary title awarded to Xun Kuang（荀况，about 313–238 B.C.), a famous thinker in the late Warring States Period.

Yang Zi（扬子）, the honorary title of Yang Xiong（扬雄，53–18 A.D.), a famous scholar in the Western Han Dynasty.

† Wen Zhong Zi（文中子）, the honorary title given to Wang Tong（王通，584–618 A.D.), a famous philosopher in the Sui Dynasty.

Lao Zi（老子）, the honorary title of Lao Dan（老聃）, the greatest thinker in the late Spring and Autumn Period. His real name was Li Er（李耳）. He was regarded as the founder of Taoism.

Zhuang Zi（庄子）, the honorary title of Zhuang Zhou（庄周，about 369–286 B.C.), a great philosopher who lived in the Warring States Period.

考世系，知终始。

自羲农，至黄帝。

号三皇，居上世。

唐有虞，号二帝。

One can proceed to historical works.

From each phase of historical evolution,

One can learn the ups and downs of each reign.

There lived Fu Xi and Shen Nong,

As well as Xuan Yuan.*

They were called the Three Emperors,

Living long before in the good old days.

Yao† and Shun‡ reigned in the later years,

Who were called the Two Emperors.

* Xuan Yuan（轩辕）, the name of the Yellow Emperor（黄帝）.

† Yao（尧）, also called Tang Yao（唐尧）, a famous emperor in pre-history China.

‡ Shun（舜）, also called Yu Shun（虞舜）, and successor to Emperor Yao, another famous emperor in pre-history China.

相揖逊，称盛世。

夏有禹，商有汤；

周文武，称三王。

夏传子，家天下。

Both yielded the crown to capable men,

And their reigns were called heydays.

There lived Yu* in the Xia Dynasty,

And there appeared Tang† in the Shang;

Together with Emperor Wen of Zhou Dynasty
  and his son‡,

They were called the Three Great Kings.

After Yu was succeeded by his son,

All under heaven were ruled by one family.

* Yu(禹), also called Yu the Great(大禹), and successor to Emperor Shun, another famous emperor in pre-history China.

† Tang (汤), also called Shang Tang(商汤), he founded the Shang Dynasty.

‡ Namely Emperor Wu of Zhou Dynasty(周武王).

四百载，迁夏社。

汤伐夏，国号商。

六百载，至纣亡。

周武王，始诛纣。

And the Xia Dynasty lasted four centuries long,
Till there was revolution in the country.
The revolution against Xia was led by Tang,
Who founded a new dynasty called Shang.
Six centuries had passed
Before it was overthrown in the reign of Zhou.
The Zhou Dynasty was founded by Emperor
Wu of Zhou Dynasty,
Who captured and beheaded cruel Zhou.

八百载，最长久。

周辙东，王纲坠。

逞干戈，尚游说。

始春秋，终战国。

The Zhou Dynasty lasted eight centuries,

The longest dynasty in history.

When the capital of Zhou was moved to the east,

The whole state began to go downward.

Seas of war broke out everywhere,

And politicians ran about canvassing.

The Eastern Zhou began with the Spring and Autumn*,

And ended with the Warring States†.

* Namely the Spring and Autumn Period, the early years of the Eastern Zhou Dynasty.

† Namely the Warring States Period, the latter period of the Eastern Zhou Dynasty.

五霸强，七雄出。

嬴秦氏，始兼并。

传二世，楚汉争。

高祖兴，汉业建。

Five dukes ruled in the former period,

And seven powers dominated in the latter.

Emperor Qin Shi Huang appeared,

And annexed all states into one empire.

When he was succeeded by his evil son*,

The Chu and the Han began to fight for the crown.

When Liu Bang won over Xiang Yu,

He, as the founder of the Han Dynasty, was called Gao Zu.

* His name is Hu Hai（胡亥）, the second son of Emperor Qin Shi Huang.

至孝平，王莽篡。

光武兴，为东汉。

四百年，终于献。

魏蜀吴，争汉鼎。

And during the reign of Emperor Xiao Ping,
The Han collapsed with Wang Mang's usurping.
The throne was restored by Liu Xiu,
Who was crowned Emperor Guang Wu.
The later four-century period is called the Eastern Han,
Ruined in the reign of Emperor Xian.
Three new states of Wei, Shu, and Wu,
Tussled fiercely for the throne of the Han.

号三国，迄两晋。

宋齐继，梁陈承。

为南朝，都金陵。

北元魏，分东西。

They were called the Three States,
To be replaced by the two Jins* in chains of wars.
The Song and the Qi rose one after another,
And the Liang and the Chen succeeded later:
They were called the Southern Dynasties as a whole,
With their capitals in Jinling City†.
Yuan founded in the north a reign of Wei,
Splitting into two sections, the east and the west.

* The Jin Dynasty was divided into two historical periods, namely the Western Jin and the Eastern Jin.

† Jinling, the old name of Nanjing.

宇文周，与高齐。

迨至隋，一土宇。

不再传，失统绪。

唐高祖，起义师。

Western Wei was renamed Northern Zhou by Yuwen Jue;

Eastern Wei was dominated by Gao Yang with the title of Northern Qi.

Not until the foundation of the Sui Dynasty

Was the whole country united.

The throne was succeeded by the son,

Who lost his life and his crown.

Li Yuan, with an imperial title of Tang Gaozu,

Rose up with his army.

除隋乱，创国基。

二十传，三百载。

梁灭之，国乃改。

梁唐晋，及汉周。

He swept away the riots and chaos,

And founded the Tang Dynasty.

With a succession of twenty emperors,

Tang lasted for three hundred years.

Before there rose the reign of the Later Liang,

Which replaced the reign of the Tang.

The Later Liang, the Later Tang, and the Later Jin,

Together with the Later Han and the Later Zhou.

称五代，皆有由。

炎宋兴，受周禅。

十八传，南北混。

辽与金，皆称帝。

Are called the Five Dynasties altogether,

Each replacing the former.

General Zhao* stood out, noble and strong,

And the emperor of the Zhou handed over his crown.

Zhao founded the Song Dynasty, with eighteen successors,

And the capital was moved southward in war riots.

Two tribes called the Liao and the Jin,

Respectively founded their imperial reigns.

* General Zhao, whose full name was Zhao Kuangyin(赵匡胤), was a general of the Later Zhou Dynasty before he founded the Song Dynasty.

元灭金，绝宋世。

莅中国，兼戎狄。

九十年，国祚废。

太祖兴，国大明。

The latter was subverted by the Yuan Dynasty,
And the Song also ended in the Yuan's invasion.
The Yuan conquered the whole country,
Together with the remote nationalities.
After a reign of ninety years,
The throne collapsed through rebellion.
When Zhu Yuanzhang distinguished himself during the uprising,
He founded a new dynasty called the Ming.

号洪武，都金陵。

迨成祖，迁燕京。

十六世，至崇祯。

权阉肆，寇如林。

He got Hong Wu as his imperial title,

And Jinling City to be the capital.

During the reign of Emperor Cheng Zu,

The capital was moved to Yanjing.

There lasted sixteen successions

Till the fatal end of Emperor Chong Zhen.

With eunuch Wei abusing the royal power,

Seas of rebellion broke out.

至李闯，神器焚。

清太祖，膺景命。

靖四方，克大定。

廿一史，全在兹。

Among them rose the Chuang King,
Who overthrew the Ming Dynasty.
Qing Taizu founded a new nation,
To fulfill the missions from Heaven.
He swept away all the enemies,
And unified the whole country.
The history of the twenty-one dynasties
Has all been mentioned above.

载治乱，知兴衰。

读史者，考实录。

通古今，若亲目。

口而诵，心而惟。

Through the reigns in order or disorder,
One can trace the ups and downs.
In studies of historical works,
One should delve into the actual records,
To grasp history on the whole,
As if shown before one's own eyes.
One can learn by reading and chanting,
And by way of meditation.

朝于斯，夕于斯。

昔仲尼，师项橐。

古圣贤，尚勤学。

赵中令，读鲁论。

One should indulge in studies

From morning till night.

Confucius set a good example,

Who once followed Xiang Tuo as a disciple.

All sages and nobles in ancient times

Would work hard at their studies.

A prime minister called Zhao Pu

Lost himself in the study of *The Analects*[*].

* Namely the *Analects of Confucius*.

彼既仕，学且勤。

披蒲编，削竹简。

彼无书，且知勉。

头悬梁，锥刺股。

Though he had a high post in the government,
He was still a diligent learner.
Lu Wenshu* copied books on a grass weave,
And Gongsun Hong† wrote on bamboo chips.
The poor guys had no books of their own,
Yet they had such means to try.
Sun Jing‡ fastened his hair to the beam,
And Su Qin§ stabbed his thighs with an awl.

* Lu Wenshu(路温舒), a prime minister of the Han Dynasty. When he was young, his family was so poor, that he had to herd sheep for the rich. During his herding, he cut cattails and wove them together in order to practice and copy writing on them.

† Gongsun Hong(公孙弘), a historical figure during the reign of Emperor Wu of the Eastern Han Dynasty. When he was in his fifties, he herded cattle for the rich. During his herding, he managed to cleave the outer skins of bamboo chips and wrote on them.

‡ Sun Jing(孙敬), a historical figure in the Eastern Han Dynasty. He attached his long hair to the overhead beam in his study when he was reading. If he dozed off, he would be awakened by the pain of his hair being pulled so that he could go on reading.

§ Su Qin(苏秦), a historical figure in the Warring States Period. He advocated that the State of Qin annex other states. When he was young, he studied very hard. He would stab his thighs with an awl to refresh himself if he felt tired.

彼不教，自勤苦。

如囊萤，如映雪。

家虽贫，学不辍。

如负薪，如挂角。

Why did both do such strange deeds?
They accepted pains to learn by themselves.
Che Yin* read under the light of glow worms,
And Sun Kang† read against the white snow.
Though they came from poor families,
They never stopped their studies.
Zhu Maichen‡ tried reading in firewood cutting,
And Li Mi§ held his book while cattle herding.

* Che Yin（车胤）, a historical figure of the Jin Dynasty. His family was so poor that he, on the summer nights, had to read in the weak glow of captured glowworms placed in a white silk bag.

† Sun Kang（孙康）, a historical figure of the Jin Dynasty. His family was poor and had no lamp. On winter nights, Sun Kang had to read against the reflection of the white snow.

‡ Zhu Maichen（朱买臣）, a famous scholar and official of the Han Dynasty.

§ Li Mi（李密）, a peasant and leader in the uprising against the Sui Dynasty. When he was young, he herded cattle for the rich. He loved reading so much so that he always hung his books on the ox horns, and would read if he was free.

身虽劳，犹苦卓。

苏老泉，二十七。

始发愤，读书籍。

彼既老，犹悔迟。

Though they were tired out at work,

They were still learning hard.

Su Xun* didn't start to learn

Until he was twenty-seven.

Though it was late for him to learn,

He finally had much to attain.

When he became old,

He still felt repentant.

* Su Xun (苏洵), a famous man of letters in the Song Dynasty. He didn't like learning when he was young, and went to great pain to learn at the age of twenty-seven.

尔小生，宜早思。

若梁灏，八十二。

对大廷，魁多士。

彼既成，众称异。

Young pupils, all of you,
Better start learning sooner.
Liang Hao* was acclaimed
At the age of eighty-two:
He stood out from the scholars,
And was listed top in the Court Examination.
Only after he had been a success,
Could others hail to him in surprise.

* Liang Hao(梁灏), a historical figure in the Song Dynasty. He took part in the imperial examination at the age of eighty-two, and was selected as *Zhuang Yuan* (the top winner in the imperial examination).

尔小生，宜立志。

莹八岁，能咏诗。

泌七岁，能赋棋。

彼颖悟，人称奇。

Young pupils, all of you,
Better decide what to do.
When Zu Ying* was eight years old,
He could recite many poems.
And when Li Mi† was seven,
He could compose a chess ode.
Such boys with unusual talents
Always surprise the other people.

* Zu Ying (祖莹), a famous scholar in the Northern Qi Dynasty.
† Li Mi (李泌), a historical figure of the Tang Dynasty.

尔幼学，当效之。

蔡文姬，能辨琴。

谢道韫，能咏吟。

彼女子，且聪敏。

Young pupils, all of you,
Better imitate what they've done.
Cai Wenji* was such a gifted girl
That she was expert at the organ.
And Xie Daoyun†, a bright young lady,
Could show her poetic gift on a snowy day.
There were many girls as such,
Who were clever and smart.

* Cai Wenji（蔡文姬）, a gifted lady of the Eastern Han Dynasty. She was famous for her talent at music.

† Xie Daoyun（谢道韫）, niece of Xie An（谢安）, a prime minister of the Eastern Jin Dynasty. Xie Daoyun was famous for her talent at poetry.

尔男子，当自警。

唐刘晏，方七岁。

举神童，作正字。

彼虽幼，身已仕。

All of you, pupil boys,

Should be aware of yourselves.

When Liu Yan*, a figure of the Tang Dynasty,

Was at the age of seven,

He was called a child sage,

In charge of proofreading books for the government.

Young as he was,

He became an official.

* Liu Yan (刘晏), a historical figure of the Tang Dynasty. He passed the imperial examination at the age of seven, and was appointed as an official in the government.

尔幼学，勉而致。

有为者，亦若是。

犬守夜，鸡司晨。

苟不学，曷为人？

All of you, young learners,

Can also achieve the same.

Whoever hold such ambition

Will also succeed like this.

A dog can keep watch at night,

And a cock can crow at dawn.

If a person fails to learn,

How can he be a successful person?

蚕吐丝，蜂酿蜜。

人不学，不如物。

幼而学，壮而行。

上致君，下泽民。

A silkworm can make silk,
And a honeybee can make honey.
If a person fails to learn,
He'll be good for nothing.
If a child learns a lot,
He'll succeed in his adulthood,
Not only serving the country,
But also benefiting the people.

扬名声，显父母。

光于前，裕于后。

人遗子，金满籝。

我教子，惟一经。

He'll run into great fame,

Bringing honor to his parents.

All his ancestors will enjoy the glory,

And all his offspring will benefit from his victory.

People usually bequeath their children

With cases of gold bars;

And what I leave to my son

Is nothing but this scripture.

勤有功，戏无益。

戒之哉，宜勉力。

Study hard, and you'll succeed;

Play truant, and you'll fail.

Be aware of all of this, behold!

And work harder and harder.

大中华文库

汉英对照

LIBRARY OF CHINESE CLASSICS

Chinese-English

千字文

THE THOUSAND CHARACTER WRITING

［梁］周兴嗣　著

Written by Zhou Xingsi

彭发胜　译注

Translated by Peng Fasheng

《千字文》简述

《千字文》是距今约1500年前，南朝梁武帝在位期间编成的，编者为梁朝散骑侍郎、给事中周兴嗣。据《梁史》以及其他一些史书记载，梁武帝为了教子读书，令一位名叫殷铁石的文学侍从，从晋代大书法家王羲之的手迹中拓下一千个不重复的字，每纸一字；但是这么多字杂乱难记，梁武帝召来自己最信赖的文学侍从周兴嗣，命其将这些字组织成一篇通俗易懂的启蒙读物。周兴嗣苦思冥想了一整夜，将这一千字联缀成一篇构思精妙、内涵丰富的四言韵书。据说，周兴嗣因用脑过度，次日已须发皆白。自此以后，《千字文》就成了一部广受欢迎的童蒙识字读本。

《千字文》每八字一行，从内容上看，可以分为四部分：第一句“天地玄黄，宇宙洪荒”至第十八句“化被草木，赖及万方”为第一部分；第十九句“盖此身发，四大五常”至第五十一句“坚持雅操，好爵自縻”为第二部分；第五十二句“都邑华夏，东西二京”至第八十一句“旷远绵邈，严岫杳冥”为第三部分；第八十二句“治本于农，务资稼穑”至倒数第二句“孤陋寡闻，愚蒙等诮”为第四部分。最后一句“谓语助者，焉哉乎也”，没有实质含义，单列出来。第一部分勾勒了宇宙形成和文化演进的概貌；第二部分重在讲述人的修养和美德，可以看出主要出于儒家的教化传统；第三部分叙述了居庙堂之高者的豪华生活和文治武功，还描述了广袤秀美的中华国土；第四部分最长，主要描述处江湖之远者的田园生活和能工巧匠的高超技艺。

在英译的过程中，译者采用了三重策略。首先是**直译**，基本上一字一词，只有少数例外，目的是为了突出原文作为识字读本的功能。**意译**部分将直译部分零散的单词重新加以组织、变换和润色，以符合英语文法和实现上下文的有机联系。另外添加的**注释**则提供了必要的背景知识，以便于英语读者理解。我们希望，通过对比直译和意译两部分，英语读者可以更好地把握汉语的特点。

About *The Thousand Character Writing*

The Thousand Character Writing was composed by Zhou Xingsi in the Liang Dynasty of the Southern Dynasties period, about 1,500 year ago. As *The History of Liang* and some other history books have it, for the purpose of educating his son, Emperor Wu ordered a scholar to copy one thousand non-repeated characters from the calligraphy of Wang Xizhi (321–379 A.D.), which was then reshuffled into a rhyming text by Zhou Xingsi. Zhou completed the exacting job overnight and found himself a white-haired man in the second morning because of intense brain work. Ever since, the essay has become one of the most popular literacy texts in China.

Eight characters a line, the essay as a whole can be divided into four parts, the first part from Line 1 to Line 18, the second from Line 19 to Line 51, the third from Line 52 to Line 81, the fourth from Line 82 to the penultimate line. Without substantial meaning, the last line is singled out. The first part outlines the cosmological process and cultural evolution in general. The second dwells upon personal upbringing and moral virtues, mostly of the Confucian tradition. The third part surveys the administrative affairs of the noble classes and the vast territory of Chinese empire. The last part, the longest also, narrates the pastoral life of common people and technical prowess of craftsmen.

In rendering this essay into English, the translator adopts a kind of triple strategy. The transliteration (TL) features one English word for one Chinese character, only with a few exceptions. It aims at highlighting the original function of the literacy text. For translation proper, words in the TL part are re-organized with some additions and alterations for grammatical propriety and contextual unity. The additional notes offer necessary background information for easier understanding. It is hoped that, by comparing TL with the translation itself, English readers may gain a better insight into the characteristics of Chinese language.

天地玄黄，

宇宙洪荒。

日月盈昃，

辰宿列张。

(TL)* sky earth black yellow,
space time flood wilderness.

The sky is black and the earth yellow; the universe was formed out of a chaotic state in the primordial time.

(TL) sun moon wax set,
star constellation arrange spread.

The sun rises and sets; the moon waxes and wanes; across the sky, constellations of stars spread.

* The transliteration (TL) features one English word for one Chinese character, only with a few exceptions.

寒来暑往，
秋收冬藏。

闰余成岁，
律吕调阳。

(**TL**) coldness come heat go,
autumn harvest winter storage.

The cold season alternates with the warm one; the crops reaped in autumn are stored in winter.

(**TL**) intercalary-month extra comprise year,
odd pitch-pipe even pitch-pipe harmonize Yang.

An intercalary month is sometimes necessary to round out a lunar year; the pitch pipes, odd and even ones together, harmonize Yin and Yang. *

* Because the lunar year of China is about ten days shorter than the usual solar year, Chinese people usually add an intercalary month to one out of three years to balance. The bamboo instrument has 12 pitch pipes of different length for an octave. Ranging from low to high, the odd pitch pipes are called lǜ and believed to represent Yang force, the even ones called lǜ are believed to reflect Yin energy. They correspond to the twelve months of the year as well.

云腾致雨，

露结为霜。

金生丽水，

玉出昆冈。

(TL) clouds rise cause rain,
dew condense make frost.

Clouds rise to end up as rain; dew are condensed into frost.

(TL) gold produce Li River,
jade crop-up Mount Kunlun.

Gold is produced in the Li River; jade crops up in Mount Kunlun. *

* The Li River, also called the Jinsha River, is in Yunnan Province; Mount Kunlun is on the southern border of Xinjiang Uygur Autonomous Region.

剑号巨阙，

珠称夜光。

果珍李柰，

菜重芥姜。

(TL) sword title Juque,
pearl call night gleam.

Of swords, the most famous was entitled Juque; of pearls, the most precious was named the Gleam of Night. *

(TL) fruit treasure plum crab-apple,
vegetable value mustard ginger.

Among fruits, plums and crab-apples are treasured; Among vegetables, mustard and ginger are valued.

* The marvelous sword was said to belong to Gou Jian (勾践, ?–465 B.C.), king of the State of Yue. After years of humiliation and suffering, he used his sword to beat his rival Fu Chai (夫差), king of the State of Wu.

海咸河淡，

鳞潜羽翔。

龙师火帝，

鸟官人皇。

(TL) sea salty river fresh,
scale swim feather fly.

The sea is salty, the river fresh; fishes swim below in water, birds fly on high in the air.

(TL) dragon master fire emperor,
bird official man sovereign.

Dragon Master, Fire Emperor, Bird Official, and Sovereign of Men are four of China's ancient rulers and officials.*

* These are four titles of China's earliest rulers and ministers. Dragon Master refers to Fu Xi（伏羲）who designated his ministers by the title of dragon; Fire Emperor to Shen Nong (神农 , Magic Farmer) who named his ministers by the title of fire. Bird Official was the title given by Shao Hao（少昊）to his officials. Sovereign of Men was the last one of the legendary "Three Sovereigns", the precedent two being Sovereign of Heaven and Sovereign of Earth.

始制文字，

乃服衣裳。

推位让国，

有虞陶唐。

(**TL**) begin invent character-writing,
then wear coat shirt.

Cang Jie, an official of the Yellow Emperor, invented character-writing; Lei Zu, wife of the Yellow Emperor, taught people the art of textile clothing.

(**TL**) yield throne pass kingdom,
You-yu Tao-tany

As to yielding the throne and government to virtuous and capable men, there were emperors like Yao and Shun.*

* Yao was the ruler of the Tao-tang Fiefdom and Shun was the Chieftain of the Youyu Clan. After long examination, Yao had full confidence in Shun and yielded his throne to him.

吊民伐罪，

周发殷汤。

坐朝问道，

垂拱平章。

(TL) condole people send-troops crime,
Zhou-Fa Yin-Tang.

To appease the oppressed people and right the wrong, Zhou Fa and Yin Tang in turn sent punitive troops against the despots.*

(TL) sit court inquire principle,
droop-clothes cup-hand peace manifest

Presiding over the court, the emperor inquired his ministers about the Way; with easy and peaceful measures, they ruled the country.†

* Zhou Fa(周发), or Ji Fa(姬发), led a punitive army against the despotic king of the Shang Dynasty and became the founding emperor of the Western Zhou Dynasty. Earlier in history, Yin Tang(殷汤), or Cheng Tang(成汤), established the Shang Dynasty after having overthrown Jie(桀) the despot of the Xia Dynasty.

† If a man stands with his clothes drooping down and hands cupped together, he is certainly in a tranquil state. The stance here signifies easy reign on the part of the emperor.

爱育黎首，

臣伏戎羌。

遐迩一体，

率宾归王。

(TL) love cultivate black head,
subjugate lay-prostrate Rong Qiang (tribes).

He cared for and sympathized with the people, and subjugated the surrounding tribes.*

(TL) far near one body,
all guest submit emperor.

Far and near, they united as one empire; all followed and submitted themselves to the emperor.

* The Rong and Qiang were two tribes to the west. Together they represented all the uncivilized tribes surrounding China in the Zhou Dynasty.

鸣凤在竹，

白驹食场。

化被草木，

赖及万方。

(TL) singing phoenix at bamboo,
white horse graze pasture.

Phoenixes sing in the bamboo grove; white horses graze in the pasture.

(TL) culture cover grass wood,
blessing reach myriad place.

Goverment of virtue benefits even the flora and fauna; the overflowing blessings reach everywhere.

盖此身发，

四大五常。

恭惟鞠养，

岂敢毁伤。

(TL) this body hair,

four essential five constant.

Our body and hair are composed of four essential elements and our behavior must conform to five constant virtues.*

(TL) respect nourishment upbringing,

how dare impair wound.

They are what our parents have nourished and raised; how dare we cause them to be impaired!

* According to Buddhist notion, the four essential elements are Earth, Water, Wind, and Fire. The five constant virtues are benevolence, righteousness, propriety, wisdom, and truthfulness in the Confucian moral system.

女慕贞洁，
男效才良。

知过必改，
得能莫忘。

(TL) woman cherish chastity purity,
man emulate talent goodness.

Women cherish pure chastity; men emulate those of wisdom and ability.

(TL) know error must rectify,
acquire cannot forget.

He who knows his own faults must rectify them; he who has acquired certain skills should constantly practice them.

罔谈彼短，
靡恃己长。

信使可覆，
器欲难量。

(TL) not talk-about other shortcoming,
not boast self excellence.

Refrain from talking about others' shortcomings, and also from bragging about your own merits.

(TL) trust must able keep,
capability endeavor difficult measure.

Words must stand the test of time; the capability for virtue should be enhanced beyond measure.

墨悲丝染，
诗赞羔羊。

景行维贤，
克念作圣。

(TL) Mo Zi grieve silk dye,
poem laud lamb.

Mo Zi grieved upon seeing white silk dyed; *The Book of Songs* glorified the lamb for the purity of its fleece.*

(TL) sublime conduct only virtuous,
constrain desire become sage.

We should respect and admire the conduct of a virtuous man; he who constrains his selfish desires becomes a sage.

* Mo Zi（墨子）was a thinker in the Warring States Period (403–221 B.C.), who founded the Mohist School, advocating "universal love and mutual benefit". His grief over the dyed silk reminds people of always maintaining innate goodness against evil influence. The white lamb lauded by *The Book of Songs* symbolizes frugality and uprightness.

德建名立，

形端表正。

空谷传声，

虚堂习听。

(TL) virtue cultivate reputation establish,
figure straight bearing correct.

With virtues cultivated, a high reputation will be established; an upright figure naturally displays dignity.

(TL) hollow valley transmit sound,
empty hall repeat listen.

A hollow valley transmits sound over a long distance; an empty and spacious hall reverberates with human voice.

祸因恶积，

福缘善庆。

尺璧非宝，

寸阴是竞。

(TL) calamity cause evil accumulate,
    happiness originate-from good reward

Calamity is caused by accumulated evils; happiness originates from kind conducts.

(TL) foot jade not treasure,
    inch shadow be fight-for.

A block of jade is no treasure whereas a blink of time is worth fighting for.

资父事君，
曰严与敬。

孝当竭力，
忠则尽命。

(TL) attend-upon father serve prince,
called respect and reverence.

Attend your parents and serve the emperor with awe and reverence.

(TL) filial-piety should exhaust effort,
loyalty may sacrifice life.

In filial piety to your parents you exert your utmost effort; in loyalty to the throne, you are willing to devote your life.

临深履薄，

夙兴温凊。

似兰斯馨，

如松之盛。

(TL) approach deep tread thin,
morning getting-up warm cool.

Always remain cautious just like approaching deep water or treading on thin ice; and you should rise early in the morning and make sure that your parents feel warm in the winter or cool in the summer.

(TL) like orchid so fragrant,
like pine-tree luxuriant.

You should cultivate virtues like those of the fragrant orchid, or like those of the luxuriant evergreen pine tree.

川流不息，
渊澄取映。

容止若思，
言辞安定。

(TL) river flow never cease,
pool clear for mirroring.

In time, your virtues will be comparable to the ever-flowing river, or to a clear mirror-like pool.

(TL) features demeanor like meditate,
words phrases calm determination.

Let your features and demeanor be like those of a thinker; and speak in a calm and determined manner.

笃初诚美，
慎终宜令。

荣业所基，
籍甚无竟。

(TL) honesty beginning indeed beautiful,
caution end worthy admirable.

Diligence in the beginning is indeed laudable; but holding on to the end is admirable even more.

(TL) glorious career thus foundation,
dependence even without limit.

When your career has a glorious foundation, it will advance beyond any limit.

学优登仕，

摄职从政。

存以甘棠，

去而益咏。

(TL) learning superior ascend official,
deputy profession administer politics.

Let learning be superior for ascending to official posts so as to participate in administrative affairs.

(TL) preserve sweet pear-tree,
gone but further hymned.

People preserved the sweet pear tree to commemorate the duke, who was gone but has been lauded ever since.*

* Early in the Zhou Dynasty, the Duke of Shao was said to conduct administrative affairs under a pear tree. Later, people preserved the tree and composed a poem to laud him.

乐殊贵贱，
礼别尊卑。

上和下睦，
夫唱妇随。

(TL) music differ noble commoner,
rites differentiate honored humble.

Music has distinctions for nobles and commoners; different uses of the rites mark the honorable and the humble.

(TL) superiors kindly inferiors peaceable,
husband call wife follow.

Superiors get along with inferiors in harmony; when the husband sings, the wife joins in chorus.

外受傅训，
入奉母仪。

诸姑伯叔，
犹子比儿。

(TL) outside obey teacher instruction,
inside observe mother rule-of-etiquette.

Outside, we obey the teacher's instructions; at home, we observe the etiquettes set up by our mothers.

(TL) those aunts uncles,
nephew comparable son.

Treat the paternal aunts and uncles like your own parents, and the nephews and nieces like your own sons and daughters.

孔怀兄弟，

同气连枝。

交友投分，

切磨箴规。

(TL) great concern elder and younger brothers,
same breathe linked branches.

Have great concern about your brothers, with whom you share the same origin of life, like branches of one tree.

(TL) make friends agreeable disposition,
carve polish admonition warning.

Make friends with those of agreeable disposition; together, you may refine and exhort each other.

仁慈隐恻，

造次弗离。

节义廉退，

颠沛匪亏。

(TL) benevolence kindness compassion sympathy, hurry not alienate.

Always maintain a benevolent and sympathetic heart; not to be alienated from it even in moments of haste.

(TL) integrity justice honesty modesty, adversity not lack.

Even in time of adversity, these virtues of integrity, justice, honesty and modesty may not be lacking.

性静情逸，

心动神疲。

守真志满，

逐物意移。

(TL) disposition tranquil emotion spontaneous,
heart ruffled spirit tired.

With a gentle disposition, one can enjoy peace; but when the heart is ruffled, the spirit becomes exhausted.

(TL) keep genuine aspiration fulfilled,
pursue thing mind distracted.

With your nature genuinely kept, your aspirations will be fulfilled; but in pursuing worldly things, the mind often becomes distracted.

坚持雅操，
好爵自縻。

都邑华夏，
东西二京。

(TL) staunchly-hold elegant virtue,
fine position of-oneself visit.

So long as you hold fast to elegant virtues, higher position will of itself visit you.

(TL) capital-city Hua-Xia (China),
east west two metropolis.

As the capital cities of the empire, there were two metropolises respectively in the east and the west.*

* The eastern metropolis was Luoyang, the western one Chang'an (now Xi'an).

背邙面洛，

浮渭据泾。

宫殿盘郁，

楼观飞惊。

(TL) behind Mount-Mang front River-Luo,
float River-Wei occupy River-Jing.

The eastern one was situated to the south of Mount Mang and in front of River Luo; the western one was adjacent to Rivers Wei and Jing.

(TL) palace hall winding dense,
tower temple fly amaze.

Palaces and halls extended in winding arrays; towers and temples soared up to one's amazement.

图写禽兽，
画彩仙灵。

丙舍傍启，
甲帐对楹。

(**TL**) picture depict bird beast,
painting color immortals spirits

There were paintings of birds and beasts, and also colorful images of immortals and spirits.

(**TL**) room-house side open,
curtain-drape facing pillar.

Houses after houses opened out on both sides; gorgeous curtains and drapes were drawn along the pillars.

肆筵设席，

鼓瑟吹笙。

升阶纳陛，

弁转疑星。

(TL) display banquet arrange mat,
strike zither blow flute

In the palace, a grand banquet was arranged; and the gala was opened to the music of zithers and flutes.

(TL) ascend terrace mount palatial-stairs,
hat whirl as if star.

When officials ascending the steps and standing before the throne, their caps wave like numerous stars.

右通广内，

左达承明。

既集坟典，

亦聚群英。

(TL) right link Guangnei-Hall,
left lead-to Chengming-Hall.

On the right, an avenue went through to the royal library; on the left, another to the national academy.*

(TL) have-assembled canons,
also gather congeries elite.

The library had assembled the canons of the Three Sovereigns and Five Emperors†; the academy had gathered literary and martial elites.

* During the Han Dynasty, Guangnei-Hall was used as the royal library, and Chengming-Hall as the national academy where scholars did researches and wrote books.

† The canons of the Three Sovereigns and Five Emperors are said to be the earliest books in the history of China.

杜稿钟隶，
漆书壁经。

府罗将相，
路侠槐卿。

(TL) Du manuscript Zhong Script,
lacquer book wall classics.

Among the collection were Du Du's cursive calligraphy and Zhong You's script, and also books written in lacquer and classics found within the double walls.*

(TL) mansion file general minister,
road flank locust-tree official.

In the court were generals and ministers standing in two lines; and the road outside was flanked by lower officials.

* Du Du (杜度) was famous for his beautiful cursive handwriting during Zhang Di's reign (76–89 A.D.) in the Han Dynasty. Likewise, Zhong You in the period of the Three Kingdoms was famed for his clerical style of calligraphy. Lacquer books were those made of bamboo chips strung together, with characters written on them in lacquer. During Prince of Lu's reign, around 150 B.C., volumes of classics were found within the double walls of Confucius' former abode in Qufu, Shandong.

户封八县，

家给千兵。

高冠陪辇，

驱毂振缨。

(TL) family grant eight county,
household give thousand soldier.

Their families had been granted eight counties; and to each house had been given a thousand soldiers.

(TL) high cap accompany imperial-chariot,
drive hub shake tassel.

In their high caps, ministers accompanied the imperial chariot; their tassels flew in the wind when the carriages rode rapidly forward.

世禄侈富，
车驾肥轻。

策功茂实，
勒碑刻铭。

(TL) generation salary lavish wealth,
chariot drive plump light.

Generations of their descendents enjoyed lavish wealth; their magnificent chariots were drawn by strong steeds.

(TL) scroll achievements substantial fact,
carve monument inscribe tablet.

Their glorious merits and virtues were recorded in scrolls, and also inscribed on stone monuments.

磻溪伊尹，

佐时阿衡。

奄宅曲阜，

微旦孰营。

(TL) Pan stream Yi Yin,
assist timely-affairs prime minister.

Lü Shang and Yi Yin, formerly lesser figures, were promoted as prime ministers to assist emperors with administrative affairs.*

(TL) State-of-Yan residence Qufu,
without Dan who manage.

To make a livable residence of Qufu in the State of Yan, if not the Duke of Dan, who could manage it?†

* Lü Shang (吕尚), or Jiang Tai Gong, had been fishing on the Pan Stream before he met Emperor Wen of Zhou Dynasty and was acknowledged as prime minister. Later, he assisted Emperor Wu of Zhou Dynasty in conquering the kingdom of Shang. Yi Yin was once a lesser official before being promoted to the prime minister position. He advised Emperor Tang of Shang Dynasty in his punitive campaign against Xia Jie the despot.

† The State of Yan, to the east of Qufu, was one of number of small areas a small county in the early years of the Zhou Dynasty. After Emperor Wu of Zhou Dynasty died, the Duke of Dan assisted his younger brother, Emperor Wen of Zhou, in building and stabilizing the Zhou Dynasty.

桓公匡合，
济弱扶倾。

绮回汉惠，
说感武丁。

(**TL**) duke-of-Huan pacify unite,
aid weak revitalize decline.

The duke of Huan pacified the uprisings and united many feudal lords; what is more, he aided the weak and revitalized the endangered.*

(**TL**) Qi return Han Hui,
Yue dream Wu Ding.

Qili Ji returned in time and restored the degraded prince; Fu Yue assisted in bringing the Shang Dynasty into prosperity.†

* The duke of Huan ranked first among the five leading feudal lords in the Spring and Autumn Period.

† Qili Ji（绮里季）was one of "Four White-headed Seniors in Mount Shang" in the Han Dynasty. They were invited into the palace to consolidate the position of the prince before he ascended the throne. After Wu Ding（武丁）, Emperor Gaozu of the Yin Dynasty, dreamt of Fu Yue（傅说）, the emperor set out to look for the man and promoted him to prime minister.

俊乂密勿，
多士寔宁。

晋楚更霸，
赵魏困横。

(TL) diligent government considerate vigilant,
many gentleman true peace.

Thanks to great governance of talented persons, the majority of people enjoyed true peace.

(TL) Jin Chu alternate hegemony,
Zhao Wei distress alliance.

Jin and Chu alternately claimed hegemony; Zhao and Wei were handicapped by the strategy of horizontal alliance.*

* Jin refers to Duke Wen of the State of Jin, Chu to King Zhuang of the State of Chu in the Spring and Autumn Period. The so-called strategy of horizontal alliance was proposed by Zhang Yi（张仪）, who advised the king of the State of Qin to seek alliance with distant states and at the same time attack its neighbors, therefore, the neighboring states of Zhao and Wei suffered from Qin's military assaults.

假途灭虢，

践土会盟。

何遵约法，

韩弊烦刑。

(TL) borrow road destroy Guo,
Jiantu meeting covenant.

A road was borrowed for the purpose of destroying the State of Guo; at Jiantu, the feudal lords met to make a covenant.*

(TL) He comply-with simplified law,
Han shortcoming heavy punishment.

Xiao He complied with the simplified laws; Han Fei suffered from his own rules of heavy punishment.†

* The road was lent by the State of Yu to Jin's troops who, in turn, destroyed the lender on their triumphant way back. At Jiantu, Wen Gong of the State of Jin once met with the feudal lords and pledged loyalty to the Zhou Dynasty.

† Xiao He (萧何) was the prime minister to the founding emperor of the Han Dynasty. Han Fei (韩非), precursor of the legislators' school, advocated rule by heavy punishment. Later, He became a sacrifice in this regard.

起翦颇牧，
用军最精。

宣威沙漠，
驰誉丹青。

(TL) Qi Jian Po Mu,

apply troops most expertly.

Those renowned generals, Bai Qi, Wang Jian, Lian Po, and Li Mu, were the best military strategists.*

(TL) declare might deserts,

riding fame painting.

Their awesome might was acknowledged even in distant deserts; their fame spread wide and passed on in paintings.

* Bai Qi（白起）and Wang Jian（王翦）were generals to the State of Qin, Lian Po（廉颇）and Li Mu（李牧）were to the State of Zhao.

九州禹迹，

百郡秦并。

岳宗泰岱，

禅主云亭。

(TL) nine state Yu footprint,
hundred prefecture Qin unify.

The nine states bore footprints of Yu the Great; and by the Primary Sovereign of Qin a hundred prefectures were unified.*

(TL) peak worship Mount Tai,
crowning-ceremony master Mount-Yun Mount-Ting.

Among the sacred peaks, the most worshiped is Mount Tai; crowning ceremonies were conducted upon Mounts Yun and Ting for generations.†

* Yu (禹) the Great devoted himself to controlling the flooding rivers all over China. The king of the State of Qin unified China and called himself "Qin Shi Huang", the Primary Sovereign of Qin. Both the "nine states" and "a hundred prefectures" refer to China in general.

† Mounts Yun and Ting are located at the foot of Mount Tai in Shandong.

雁门紫塞，

鸡田赤诚。

昆池碣石，

钜野洞庭。

(TL) wild-goose gate purple pass,
chicken field red city.

In China, there are places as such: the Wild-Goose Pass in the west, the Great Wall in the north, the distant Jitian beyond the northwestern outpost, and Mount Chicheng in the southeast.

(TL) Kun pool Mount-Jieshi,
(lake) Juye Dongting.

Also, Kunming Lake in Yunnan Province and Mounts Jieshi in Hebei, and the lakes of Juye and Dongting in Shandong and Hunan respectively.

旷远绵邈，

岩岫杳冥。

治本于农，

务兹稼穑。

(TL) remote distant extend afar,
cliff cave far-off dark.

Over the vast territory, there are beautiful rivers and mountains majestic cliffs and caves.

(TL) government root in agriculture,
occupation sowing reaping.

Good government is rooted in agriculture, with which the people are occupied, sowing and reaping.

俶载南亩，

我艺黍稷。

税熟贡新，

劝赏黜陟。

(TL) begin work southern field,

I art millet sorghum.

Now, beginning my cause in the southern fields, I am an expert in farming millet and sorghum.

(TL) tax ripe pay new,

exhort reward demote promote.

In harvest season, tax is paid on the newly-reaped grain; the politics has balanced exhortation and reward, demotion and promotion.

孟轲敦素，

史鱼秉直。

庶几中庸，

劳谦谨敕。

(TL) Meng Ke esteem simplicity,
history fish tenacious straightforward.

Mencius advocated simplicity; Minister Shi Yu was known to be tenacious and straightforward.*

(TL) almost nearly golden-mean,
hard-working modest discreet self-critical.

Never stay from the rule of the Golden Mean; be always hardworking, modest, discreet, and self-critical.

* Mencius (ca. 372–289), or Meng Ke, was a great Confucian thinker in the Warring States Period. Shi Yu was a minister of the State of Wei in the Spring and Autumn Period.

聆音察理，

鉴貌辨色。

贻厥嘉猷，

勉其祗植。

(TL) listen voice investigate reason,

examine appearance discriminate features.

When listening to speech, investigate the reason behind what is said; in social contact, keep a discerning eye on people's appearances.

(TL) bequeath one's excellent plan,

encourage one's respectful establishment.

Bequeath your children excellent advice and plans of action; and encourage them to develop respectful establishments.

省躬讥诫，
宠增抗极。

殆辱近耻，
林皋幸即。

(TL) reexamine oneself ridicule admonition,
favor increase against extremity.

In the face of ridicules and admonitions, make a point of examining yourself; when favors increasingly come in, keep them from extremity lest the fortune would decline.

(TL) danger disgrace near shame,
forest upland happy dwell.

When disgrace looms or shame is near, a wooded retreat may promise you a happy life.

两疏见机，

解组谁逼。

索居闲处，

沉默寂寥。

(TL) two Shu discern opportunity,
untie seal-ribbon who press.

The two Shu timely discerned the opportunity of resignation; who might press them in their hermitage?*

(TL) solitary living idle dwelling,
quiet silent unmolested.

In a remote forest, they lived a quiet and unbothered life.

* The two Shu were Shu Guang（疏广）and his nephew Shu Shou（疏受）in the Han Dynasty.

求古寻论，

散虑逍遥。

欣奏累遣，

戚谢欢招。

(TL) see ancient scrutinize discourse,

dismiss anxiety careless roam.

Time was spent in reading the works of the ancients; so as to delve into the philosophy of life and dismiss anxiety.

(TL) joy converge care banish,

grief refuse gladness beckon.

Let joys converge, and worries diminish; troubles dissipate, and gladness beckon.

渠荷的历，

园莽抽条。

枇杷晚翠，

梧桐蚤凋。

(TL) canal lotus washed brilliance,
garden undergrowth sprout twig

In summer, lotus flowers in the canal bloom brilliant; in springtime, plants in the garden sprout new twigs.

(TL) loquat late green,
wutong-tree early wither.

The loquat remains green late in winter; the phoenix tree sheds leaves early in autumn.

陈根委翳，

落叶飘摇。

游鹍独运，

凌摩绛霄。

(TL) old root sinuous shade,
falling leaf fly sway.

Old trees of sinuous roots still provide dense shade, though some of their leaves are falling in blighting wind.

(TL) rove kun alone glide,
soar-up touch scarlet empyrean.

The roving bird Kun-Peng glides in the sky alone, and soars up to touch the empyrean of rosy clouds.*

* Kun-Peng is a gigantic bird in Chinese legend, symbolizing lofty aspiration and determined will.

耽读玩市，

寓目囊箱。

易輶攸畏，

属耳垣墙。

(TL) lost-in reading play market-place,
full eye sack box.

The philosopher was lost in reading even in the noisy market; what occupied his mind were sacks and boxes of books.*

(TL) change light-chariot toward fear,
belong ear wall.

Speaking lightly and recklessly is to be guarded against, because eavesdroppers may lurk behind the wall.

* The philosopher was Wang Chong (王充，ca.27–97), living in the then capital city Luoyang.

具膳餐饭，

适口充肠。

饱饫烹宰，

饥厌糟糠。

(TL) prepare cuisine meal rice,
suit mouth stuff intestines.

We prepare rice and dishes just to suit our appetite and stuff our stomachs.

(TL) full surfeit boil slaughter,
hungry satisfy dregs chaff.

In good times, we may surfeit ourselves with delicious meat; in poor days, dregs and chaff bring no less content.

亲戚故旧，
老少异粮。

妾御绩纺，
侍巾帷房。

(TL) family relative friend,
old young different food.

Warmly receive your relatives and friends; let the old and the young be treated with different kinds of food.

(TL) concubine attend-to spinning weaving,
wait-upon towel drape bedroom.

The wife attends to spinning and weaving, and waits upon her husband in the bedroom.

纨扇圆絜，

银烛炜煌。

昼眠夕寐，

蓝笋象床。

(TL) silk fan round clean,
silvery candle gleam glow.

The silk fan is like a full moon, bright and elegant; the flames on silver candlesticks gleam and glow.

(TL) daytime nap nighttime sleep,
blue bamboo-shoot ivory bed.

For daytime naps and nighttime sleep, there are blue bamboo mats and ivory-decorated beds.

弦歌酒宴，
接杯举觞。

矫手顿足，
悦豫且康。

(TL) string song wine feast,
take cup lift goblet.

To the sound of stringed instruments and songs, people feast on wine, raising cups and goblets and drinking to their fill.

(TL) wave hand stomp foot,
joyous and healthy.

They cannot help waving their hands and stomping their feet, so joyous and healthy.

嫡后嗣续，

祭祀烝尝。

稽颡再拜，

悚惧恐惶。

(TL) lineal descendant heir continue,
sacrificial-ceremony in-winter in-autumn.

Lineal descendants continue the heredity; they offer sacrificial ceremonies to their ancestors in four seasons.

(TL) kowtow repeat bowing,
fearful awful apprehensive worried.

They worship their ancestors by kowtowing, their heart immersed in respectful apprehension.

笺牒简要，
顾答审详。

骸垢想浴，
执热愿凉。

(TL) letter document concise to-the-point,
face-to-face reply well-considered detailed.

In writing letters or documents, be concise and to the point; but replies to inquiries must be well-considered and detailed.

(TL) body dirty think-of bathing,
handle hot wish cool.

When the body is dirty, one thinks of bathing; when handling something hot, one wishes it was cool.

驴骡犊特，

骇跃超骧。

诛斩贼盗，

捕获叛亡。

(TL) donkey mule calf bull,
startled leap gallop prance.

Donkeys, mules, calves, and bulls; when startled, they leap and prance.

(TL) execute behead thief burglar,
arrest seize rebel fugitive.

Thieves and burglars are punished or executed; rebels and fugitives seized and arrested.

布射僚丸，

嵇琴阮啸。

恬笔伦纸，

钧巧任钓。

(TL) Bu shooting Liao ball,
Ji zither Ruan whistle.

Skillful was Lü Bu in shooting arrows, Yi Liao juggling balls; artistic was Ji Kang with the zither, Ruan Ji in whistling.*

(TL) Tian brush Lun paper,
Jun skill Ren angling.

Meng Tian invented the writing brush, Cai Lun paper; Ma Jun was a skillful craftsman, Ren Gongzi an expert at fishing.†

* Lü Bu（吕布）was a general at the end of the Eastern Han Dynasty, famed for archery. Yi Liao（宜僚）was a man in the State of Chu, good at juggling balls. Both Ji Kang（嵇康）and Ruan Ji（阮籍）were among the "Seven Worthy Men in the Bamboo Grove", living in the period of the Three Kingdoms.

† Meng Tian（蒙恬）was a general in the State of Qin in the Warring States Period. Cai Lun（蔡伦）was a court official in the Eastern Han Dynasty. Ma Jun（马钧）, living in the period of the Three Kingdoms, invented many mechanical devices. Ren Gongzi（任公子）was a fictitious person in Zhuangzi's work.

释纷利俗，

并皆佳妙。

毛施淑姿，

工颦妍笑。

(TL) relieve trouble benefit vulgar,
together all marvelous admirable.

They relieved people of troubles and were beneficial to the world; all of them were marvelous and admirable.

(TL) Mao Shi demure beauty,
artful frowning beautiful smile.

Xi Shi and Mao Qiang were demure beauties; the former could artfully knit her brows, the latter glowed with enchantiny smiles.*

* Mao Qiang（毛嫱）and Xi Shi（西施）were celebrated beauties in ancient China.

年矢每催，

曦晖朗曜。

璇玑悬斡，

晦魄环照。

(TL) year arrow every urge,
dawn sunshine bright blaze.

Years fly at an arrow's speed, one pushing on the other; but the sun always blazes bright.

(TL) Cynosure suspend revolve,
moon cycle shine.

The Big Dipper revolves with the seasons; the moon waxes and wanes in its cyclic movement.

指薪修祜，

永绥吉劭。

矩步引领，

俯仰廊庙。

(TL) finger firewood cultivate blessing,
forever peace auspicious laudable.

In the way of "fat as firewood", fortunes are passed on to our descendents; what we wish for are lasting peace and happiness.*

(TL) square pace stretch neck,
look-down look-up corridor temple.

With even pace and straight head, the officials confidently handle imperical orders.

* The English equivalent of *zhi* (指) is finger, but here in this association, it is believed to be a mistaken form of a similar character *zhi* (脂) meaning "fat", because the phrase "fat as firewood" comes from the third chapter of Zhuangzi's work. The original text reads: "Used as firewood, the fat will burn out in the end. But if the fire passes on from one piece to the next, it will never extinguish."

束带矜庄，

徘徊瞻眺。

孤陋寡闻，

愚蒙等诮。

(TL) belt girdle dignified serious,
walk-to-and-fro gaze distant-look.

Being properly dressed enhances our your weight and dignity; then you walk in measured steps.

(TL) secluded rustic meager learning,
foolish illiterate equal mock.

Those of half knowledge, the foolish and the illiterate, all alike are open to jeer and sneer.

谓语助者，

焉哉乎也。

(TL) say speak auxiliary particle,
yan zai hu ye.

The auxiliary particles are yan, zai, hu, and ye, for interrogation, amazement, exclamation and for winding up a sentence.

大中华文库

汉英对照

LIBRARY OF CHINESE CLASSICS

Chinese-English

孝 经

THE BOOK OF FILIAL PIETY

顾丹柯 译注

Translated by Gu Danke

《孝经》简述

《孝经》是儒家经典《十三经》中的一种，是专门谈“孝”的一部著作。与《十三经》中其他十二经不同的是，它在成书之初便以“经”来命名，而其他十二经则是由后人归入“经”的行列，可见其在《十三经》中的特殊性和重要性。

关于《孝经》的作者，有孔子说，有曾参说，有孔子弟子说，有曾参弟子说，有子思（曾参弟子、孔子孙）说，有孟子说，更有人认为《孝经》乃后人伪作。总而言之，关于《孝经》作者，众说纷纭，莫衷一是，尚无定论。至于《孝经》的成书年代，据有的学者研究，《吕览》中有多处引用《孝经》，因此认为比较确切的说法是先于《吕览》，成书于先秦。

《孝经》有“古今文”《古文孝经》和《今文孝经》之别。秦始皇“焚书坑儒”,《孝经》亦在被禁之列，但有人冒险收藏，至汉时献出。为了传授之便，有学者用隶书重写，后人称《今文孝经》。而《古文孝经》，据说是汉景帝之子鲁恭王从孔子古宅旧墙中发现的。是书用先秦籀文写成，故称《古文孝经》。两书内容有异，西汉刘向以《今文孝经》为主本，以《古文孝经》为参考，整理厘定，凡十八章，1800字左右，流传至今。

《孝经》是一部专门阐述“孝道”的书，强调“夫孝，天之经也”。民间也有“百善孝为先”的说法。曾参对“孝道”有更明确的说法:“孝有三：大孝尊亲，其次弗辱，其下能养。”

（《礼记·祭义》）虽然《孝经》认为人的品德的根本是对父母克尽孝道，但其核心却不尽讲孝，而在以“孝”劝“忠”，要做到在家行孝，出门尽忠，忠于君主。《孝经》在中国伦理思想中，首次将孝亲与忠君联系起来，认为“孝”是“忠”的基础，“忠”是“孝”的发展和延伸。正因为如此，《孝经》引起了历代君王的极大关注，不少帝王都为《孝经》作注作疏，其中最为著名的要数唐玄宗李隆基的《孝经注》。

我们现在了解、学习《孝经》，应该采取实事求是、尊重历史的态度，而不是盲目尊崇或盲目否定；应该将重点放在其伦理学的价值上，而不是拘泥于具体的细节；应该从宏观的角度来理解儒家“孝道”对当今社会生活的启迪意义，而不是不假思索的一味照搬或一味摈弃。注意这些问题，对我们创建和谐社会是大有好处的。

About *The Book of Filial Piety*

The Book of Filial Piety is one of the Confucian *Shi San Jing*, or the *Thirteen Confucian Classics*, and the only one on "filial piety". *Jing* in Chinese means "Canon", and what makes the book unique is that it was entitled the *Canon of Filial Piety*, while the other twelve books were not canons when they were written, but were categorised as canons by later scholars. So it's not difficult for us to see the particularity and significance of the book.

Scholars' opinions differ on the authorship of the book. Some maintain that it was written by Confucius himself, others by Zeng Shen, Confucius' disciple, still others by Confucius' other disciples or Zeng Shen's disciples, or by Zi Si, Confucius' grandson and Zeng Shen's disciple, or even by Mencius. Some even said that it was a pseudograph by later generations. In a word, nobody is certain as to who really wrote it. As for the details of time the book was finished, there are also different versions. But some scholars say that they have found quite a few citations from *The Book of Filial Piety* in the *Historical Writings Compiled by Lü Buwei*, so it is safe to say that it was written in the pre-Qin period, before *Historical Writings Compiled by Lü Buwei*.

The Book of Filial Piety has two versions: the *Old Text* and the *New Text*. Qin Shi Huang, or the First Emperor of the Qin Dynasty, burned books and buried Confucian scholars alive. *The Book of Filial Piety* was also among those to be burned, but somebody ran the risk of preserving it, and did not take it out until the Han Dynasty. For the sake of easier circulation and instruction, some scholar or scholars took the trouble to rewrite it in the then prevailing official script, and it came to be known as the *New Text*. The *Old Text* is said to have been discovered in the old house of Confucius by Liu Fei, Prince of Lu and son of the Han Dynasty Emperor Jing. This book was written in the script of the pre-Qin big seal characters, thus gaining the name of the *Old Text*. There are differences in the two books. In the Western Han Dynasty, Liu Xiang, using the *New Text* as a foundation and with the *Old Text* as reference, produced a fair copy of the book with more than 1,800 Chinese characters in 18 chapters, which has come down to the present day.

The Book of Filial Piety is one that elaborates on filial piety, laying stress on that "*filial piety is the constant law of Heaven*". There was also a popular saying in ancient China: "*Filial piety is the most important of all virtues.*" Zeng Shen had his more definite statement on filial piety, "*Of the three ways of filial piety, the greatest is to respect one's parents, the next is not to put one's parents to shame, and the bottommost is to support one's parents financially.*" Much as *The Book of Filial Piety* maintains that the fundamental virtue of man is to be filial to one's parents, it is to advocate "being loyal" with "filial piety" at the core: one has to be filial to one's parents at home, but when out, he should be loyal to the sovereign. *The Book of Filial Piety*, as a book of traditional Chinese thought of ethics, is the very first one that related filial piety one's parents to loyalty to the sovereign, and stressed that "filial piety" is the foundation of "loyalty", and "loyalty" is the development and elongation of "filial piety". Because of this, *The Book of Filial Piety* captured the attention of many kings or emperors, quite a few of whom annotated or interpreted *The Book of Filial Piety*, of which the most famous was the Tang Dynasty Emperor Li Longji's *Exegesis of The Book of Filial Piety*.

When we get to know and learn *The Book of Filial Piety* now, we must adopt the attitude of being practical and respecting history instead of showing unbridled worship; we must lay emphasis on its ethical value instead of being scrupulous about minor details; we should try to understand the enlightening significance of Confucian "filial piety" with regard to present-day social life instead of indiscriminate imitation or disdainful rejection. It will be of great benefit to the construction of a harmonious society if we keep these in mind.

目　录

开宗明义章第一　240
天子章第二　244
诸侯章第三　246
卿、大夫章第四　248
士章第五　252
庶人章第六　254
三才章第七　256
孝治章第八　260
圣治章第九　264
纪孝行章第十　270
五刑章第十一　274
广要道章第十二　276
广至德章第十三　280
广扬名章第十四　282
谏争章第十五　284
感应章第十六　288
事君章第十七　292
丧亲章第十八　294

CONTENTS

Chapter I
Introduction to the Theme and Significance of the Book 241

Chapter II
The Filial Piety of the Son of Heaven 245

Chapter III
The Filial Piety of Feudal Princes 247

Chapter IV
The Filial Piety of Ministers and Senior Officials 249

Chapter V
The Filial Piety of Petty Officers 253

Chapter VI
The Filial Piety of the Common People 255

Chapter VII
The Three Powers 257

Chapter VIII
Government with Filial Piety 261

Chapter IX
Governance by the Sages 265

Chapter X
An Account of Practising Filial Piety 271

Chapter XI
The Five Punishments 275

Chapter XII
The Elucidation of the Most Important Principle 277

Chapter XIII
The Elucidation of the Greatest Virtue 281

Chapter XIV
Leaving a Good Name to Posterity 283

Chapter XV
Frank Persuasion and Remonstrance 285

Chapter XVI
Interaction Between Gods and Mankind 289

Chapter XVII
Serving the King 293

Chapter XVIII
Mourning for Deceased Parent 295

开宗明义章第一

仲尼居，曾子侍。

子曰：先王有至德要道，以顺天下，民用和睦，上下无怨。汝知之乎？

曾子避席曰：参不敏，何足以知之？

子曰：夫孝，德之本也，教之所由生也。复坐，吾语汝。

身体发肤，受之父母，不敢毁伤，孝之始也；立身行道，扬名于后世，以显父母，孝之终也。

夫孝，始于事亲，中于事君，终于立身。

《大雅》云："无念尔祖，聿修厥德。"

■白话译文

孔子闲居在家，他的学生曾参在旁陪坐。

CHAPTER I

INTRODUCTION TO THE THEME AND SIGNIFICANCE OF THE BOOK

Zhongni, or Confucius, was at home, unoccupied, and Zeng Zi, or Zeng Shen, was sitting at his side, attending to him.

Confucius said, "The ancient kings applied the greatest virtue and the most important principle to make the common people submit to them. The people lived in harmony, and there were no complaints or grievances between the ruling and the ruled. Do you know how this could be?"

Zeng Zi stood up from his mattress seat and replied, "I am not that wise, so how would I be able to understand that?"

Confucius expounded, "It is filial piety. It is the very foundation of all virtues, from which all enlightenment for the common people are generated. Go back and sit down, and I will tell you why."

"Our physical bodies, hair and skin, are all bestowed upon us by our parents, so we should not dare to injure or hurt them, and that is the starting point of filial piety. If you establish yourself in society successfully, your name will be passed down to later generations, and your parents will be honoured. That is the ultimate point of filial piety."

"Therefore, filial piety begins from your love for your parents, continues to show your loyalty to your superiors, and ends up in establishing yourself in society."

孔子说：过去圣帝明君，有最美好的道德和最精要的道理，使天下人心归顺，百姓和睦。不管高贵与卑贱，从上到下无人心怀怨恨。你知道这是为什么吗？

曾参离开自己的坐席，站起来说：我不够聪明，怎么会知道呢！

孔子说：是孝。孝是一切德行的根本，一切教化都是由它而产生的。你回原席坐下，我跟你说。

人的躯体、四肢、毛发和皮肤，都是父母给的，不敢使它有任何毁坏和伤害，这是孝的开始。提高自身修养，奉行道义，扬名于后世，使父母觉得有光彩、荣耀，这是孝的终极目标。

孝啊，从侍奉父母亲开始，然后是为君王效忠，最后是建立功名、光宗耀祖。

《诗经·大雅》中说："怎么可以不思念你的先祖呢？要努力弘扬先祖的美德啊！"

The "Major Court Hymn" of *The Book of Songs* says, "Do not forget your ancestors, and cultivate yourself with their virtue."

Translator's Notes

1. *The Book of Filial Piety* is one of the 13 Confucian classics or canons. The uniqueness of the book is that it was named a canon when it first appeared, though here I just use the word "Book" in the English title — *The Book of Filial Piety*. From this, you can easily know the importance of the book in the Confucian tradition.
2. This chapter serves as an introduction that presents the gist or highlight of the book, and all the other chapters that follow are detailed elaborations or interpretations of this chapter. Filial piety starts with the love of their own physical bodies (including "*shen*" the torso, "*ti*" the limbs, "*fa*" hair, and "*fu*" skin), as they were given by their parents, and ends with their success in society, so that their names could be passed down to and remembered by later generations, which would add honour and glory to their parents and ancestors.
3. Apart from the treatment of filial piety to one's parents and respect for one's brothers, the concept of "loyalty" to the sovereign or to the superior is also put forward. So we can see that, according to Confucianism, filial piety and loyalty are so closely related to each other that they cannot be treated separately. This will become clearer when you read the subsequent chapters.
4. It is true that the Chinese people lay much stress on filial piety, but it does not mean that people of other countries or nations are not filial, though they may show their filial piety in ways different from the Chinese. For instance, the fifth of the "Ten Commandments" of the Holy Bible says, "Honour your father and your mother." You may well say this is filial piety expressed in a different way.

天子章第二

子曰：爱亲者，不敢恶于人；敬亲者，不敢慢于人。爱敬尽于事亲，而德教加于百姓，刑于四海。盖天子之孝也。

《甫刑》云："一人有庆，兆民赖之。"

白话译文

孔子说：能够爱自己父母的人，就会以这种爱心对待别人的父母，不会厌恶他们。能够尊敬自己父母的人，就会以这种尊敬之心爱敬别人的父母，不会怠慢他们。以爱和尊敬的态度尽心尽力地侍奉父母，而将德行和教化施加于普通老百姓，给天下老百姓树立了榜样，他们就会效法，这就是天子的孝道呀。

《甫刑》里说："天子一人有善行，广大老百姓就可以依靠他了。"

CHAPTER II

THE FILIAL PIETY OF THE SON OF HEAVEN

Confucius said, "If the Son of Heaven, i.e., the sovereign, loves his parents, he will not detest the parents of others. If he respects his parents, he will not maltreat the parents of others. The Son of Heaven treats his parents with love and respect, leaving a great impact on his subjects with his ultimate virtue, thus setting a worthy example for the common people. That is the filial piety of the Son of Heaven."

"Marquis Fu on Punishments" in *The Book of Documents* says, "If the Son of Heaven is committed to virtuous deeds, the common people can rely on him."

Translator's Notes

1. From this chapter to the next four chapters, five types of filial piety are dealt with according to different social status, from the highest to the lowest, with each chapter focusing on one type. In this chapter, the filial piety of the Son of Heaven, that is, the king or the emperor, is discussed. No matter what the Son of Heaven's social status is, he is also a son with parents, so he should shoulder filial duty like anybody else.
2. To the Son of Heaven, filial piety is not simply the love and respect for his own parents, he should also love and respect all the parents of all the people he governs. Otherwise, it would be impossible for him to be a qualified and responsible sovereign. In addition, if the Son of Heaven was filial and dutiful, the common people would think that he was trustworthy, and would support him and count on him.

诸侯章第三

在上不骄，高而不危；制节谨度，满而不溢。高而不危，所以长守贵也；满而不溢，所以长守富也。富贵不离其身，然后能保其社稷，而和其民人。盖诸侯之孝也。

《诗》云：“战战兢兢，如临深渊，如履薄冰。”

白话译文

诸侯身居高位而不骄傲，位虽高也不会有危险；厉行节约，严格遵守法度，财富充盈也不会被滥用。地位高而没有危险，就能长久保持尊贵的地位；财富充盈却没有被滥用，就能长久保持富足。

自身拥有富贵，才能保住自己的国家，人民才能和睦安宁，这就是诸侯的孝道。

《诗经》说：“凡事要小心谨慎，（要有危机感，）就像身临深渊，或脚踩薄冰一样。”

CHAPTER III

THE FILIAL PIETY OF FEUDAL PRINCES

If the feudal prince is not conceited, he will not be endangered in spite of his high position. If he can practise thrift and respect the laws, he will not be corrupted in face of the nation's wealth. Holding the high position without being endangered, he can long retain the esteem of being a feudal prince; in charge of the nation's wealth without being extravagant and corrupt, he can long retain the wealth of the nation.

If he can retain the nation's wealth and honour, he will protect the nation itself, and will be on harmonious terms with the common people. And that is the filial piety of the feudal prince.

The Book of Songs says, "In great place, you should feel fear and trepidation, like standing upon the edge of an abyss or treading on thin ice."

Translator's Notes

1. This chapter deals with the filial duty of a feudal prince. He has a social status higher than all the others except the emperor. In the early days of the Western Zhou Dynasty (1046–771), feudal princes were classified into five ranks in accordance with their relationship with the emperor and the achievements in their service: the duke, the marquis, the earl, the viscount, and the baron.
2. The filial piety on the part of a feudal prince is to behave in a proper and modest way, to strictly follow the law, and to practise economy. In that case, he will be able to protect the country, and be on good terms with the people.

卿、大夫章第四

非先王之法服不敢服，非先王之法言不敢道，非先王之德行不敢行。是故非法不言，非道不行。口无择言，身无择行，言满天下无口过，行满天下无怨恶。三者备矣，然后能守其宗庙。盖卿、大夫之孝也。

《诗》云：“夙夜匪懈，以事一人。”

白话译文

不符合先王礼法的衣服卿、大夫不敢穿，不符合先王礼法的话卿、大夫不敢说，不符合先王德行的事卿、大夫不敢做。因此，不合礼法的话不说，不合德行的事不做。这样，说的话没有不合礼法的，做的事没有不合德行的。话说得再多，也不会说错话，事做得再多，也不会使别人怨恨你。这三样（衣着、说话、德行）都做好了，就可以守住其宗庙。这就是卿、大夫的孝。

《诗经》说：“早晚都不敢懈怠，竭尽全力侍奉天子一人。”

CHAPTER IV

THE FILIAL PIETY OF MINISTERS AND SENIOR OFFICIALS

The robes not prescribed apt for the ranks by the ancient king, ministers and senior officials dare not wear; the utterances not prescribed appropriate for the rites by the ancient king, ministers and senior officials dare not utter; and the deeds not prescribed proper for morality by the ancient king, ministers and senior officials dare not do. Therefore, ministers and senior officials should not wear what is not right for the rites, and not do what is not right for the rites. To the ministers and senior officials, they should not say anything that is offensive and improper, nor do anything that is offensive and improper. If your robes, utterances and conduct are in conformity with what the ancient king prescribed, you will be able to keep your family temples. And that is the filial piety of a minister and senior official.

The Book of Songs says, "From morning till evening, you should serve the king with untiring efforts and devotion."

Translator's Notes

1. This chapter is about the filial piety of *qing* (ministers) and *dafu* (senior officials), who were both high officials in feudal China. What they were to do

was do everything appropriately according to the right rituals designated by the ancient kings or emperors, including the ways of dressing themselves, of speaking, and of behaving. Only in this way could they win the appraisal of the common people and retain their ancestral temples. This again certifies the close relationship between filial piety and loyalty.

2. What is discussed in this chapter seems to be too remote to be relevant to the people of the 21st century, but, in fact, it is as useful as it was in the past, if we change the "ancient king" into the "law". For modern man, whether you are Chinese, British, Japanese, or a citizen of any other country, the law is the "bottom line" that should not be ignored.

士章第五

资于事父以事母，而爱同；资于事父以事君，而敬同。故母取其爱，而君取其敬，兼之者父也。故以孝事君则忠，以敬事长则顺。忠顺不失，以事其上，然后能保其禄位，而守其祭祀。盖士之孝也。

《诗》云：“夙兴夜寐，无忝尔所生。”

白话译文

用像给予父亲的爱一样爱母亲，用像对待父亲的敬一样敬君王，所以，对待母亲主要是爱，对待君王主要是敬，而对待父亲则是爱和敬兼而有之。因此，用对待父亲的孝心侍奉君王就是忠君，用对待兄长的敬重侍奉长官就是顺从。对君王的忠和对上级的顺都做到没有过失，就能保住其禄位、守住其祭祀。这就是仕的孝。

《诗经》说：“要起早贪黑（努力工作），不要让生养你的人（父母）蒙羞。”

CHAPTER V

THE FILIAL PIETY OF PETTY OFFICERS

Love his own mother in the same way he loves his own father, respects his king in the same way he respects his own father, so the right attitude towards his own mother is love, and the right attitude towards his king is respect, but for his own father he should show both love and respect. Therefore, the filial piety for the king is loyalty, and the respect for the seniors is docility. If he can serve his king with loyalty and his seniors with docility, he will keep his emolument and position, and the right to offer sacrifices for the ancestors of his family. And that is the filial piety of *shi*, or a petty officer.

The Book of Songs says, "Rise early and retire late, so as not to humiliate your parents."

Translator's Notes

1. *Shi* in Chinese has at least three meanings: a soldier, a scholar, or an official of low ranks. Here, it means the third, that is, the petty officer.
2. A *shi* or petty officer was only higher in social status than the common people, and his filial piety was shown in his conduct towards his superiors, including his father and mother.

庶人章第六

用天之道，分地之利，谨身节用，以养父母。此庶人之孝也。

故自天子至于庶人，孝无终始，而患不及者，未之有也。

白话译文

好好利用大自然的规律，搞清楚土地的情况，洁身谨慎，生活节俭，以此来奉养父母。这是平民百姓的孝。

因此，不管是天子，还是平民，行孝是无始无终的事，担心自己做不到孝，那是从来没有的。

CHAPTER VI

THE FILIAL PIETY OF THE COMMON PEOPLE

(The common people should) make good use of the laws of nature, know the advantages and disadvantages of the land, and be prudent in their deeds so as to support their parents. That is the filial piety of the common people.

Therefore, from the Son of Heaven down to the common people, whether noble or humble, all can be dutiful to their parents, as filial piety is everlasting, without beginning or ending. The apprehension about not being dutiful to their parents is never seen.

Translator's Notes

1. The average people had no ranks at all. They lived a life, which was closest to nature, with the change of seasons, and with the rising and setting of the sun. Their filial piety was to take advantage of the natural resources, work hard in the fields, so that they were able to support their parents and raise children.
2. By now, all the five types of filial piety have been covered. Whether you are a king, a high official, a petty clerk, or even an average person with no social status at all, you are able to be filial. Filial piety is universal, and denies no nation, no skin colour, and no individual. Who shuts filial piety out shall be, in turn, shut from filial piety.

三才章第七

曾子曰：甚哉！孝之大也。

子曰：夫孝，天之经也，地之义也，民之行也。天地之经，而民是则之。则天之明，因地之利，以顺天下。是以其教不肃而成，其政不严而治。

先王见教之可以化民也，是故先之以博爱，而民莫遗其亲；陈之于德义，而民兴行。先之以敬让，而民不争；导之以礼乐，而民和睦；示之以好恶，而民知禁。

《诗》云："赫赫师尹，民具尔瞻。"

白话译文

曾子说：了不起啊！孝道多么伟大！

孔子说：孝啊，是上天运行的法则，是大地生息的力量，是每个人行为的准则。正因为它是天之理、地之力，人们就效法它。用此（天明、地利）来使天、地、人"三才"贯通，使

CHAPTER VII

THE THREE POWERS

Zeng Zi said, "How great filial piety is!"

Confucius expounded, "Filial piety, like the constant law of Heaven and the generating power of Earth, is the criterion of human conduct. As it is the law of Heaven and the power of Earth, human beings observe it. In imitation of Heaven's law and the Earth's power, the king earns the trust of the people, in spite of his indulgent moralisation, he succeeds; and in spite of his lenient administration, he governs."

"The ancient king saw that moralisation could enlighten the common people, so he took the initiative to practise universal love, and there was no more abandonment of parents; he elaborated on the significance of morality and virtue, and the people loved to follow; he showed respect and modesty, and there were no conflicts among the people; he introduced rites and music, and the people lived in harmony; he sorted the good out from the evil, and the people become aware of what is prohibited by the law."

The Book of Songs says, "Grave and eminent Master Yin, all the people are watching you."

天下百姓顺从。

先王（夏禹、商汤、周文王、周武王等）发现百姓接受教化，可以使他们逐渐转化，因此，就带头实行博爱，从而百姓受到影响，再没有人遗弃自己的亲人了。向百姓陈说道德义理，百姓自己也就自觉讲道德，行义举；带头尊重他人，相互礼让，百姓也就不再相互争夺。用礼乐引导影响，则百姓和睦相处，明示什么是好的、什么是恶的，百姓就明白哪些能做，哪些不能做。

《诗经》说："名声赫赫的太师尹氏啊，人民都景仰你呀！"

Translator's Notes

1. Heaven, Earth, and Man are called *san cai*, or the "three powers". What is the relationship between the three powers? *Cai* in Chinese indicates power. The power of Heaven is Constancy, the power of Earth is Gestation, and the power of Man is Filial Piety. Of all human conducts, filial piety is the primary, the greatest, and the most important, therefore, its power is limitless and boundless, like the constancy of Heaven and the gestation of Earth.
2. The phrase *bo ai*, or "universal love" can be easily translated into, but, in fact, is not the same as "philanthropy". Philanthropy means "the effort or inclination to increase the well-being of humankind, as by charitable aid or donations", and is more like the Mohist term of *jian ai*, or "love without distinction". The Confucian "universal love" is based on "filial piety". That is to say, people's love should be classified into some progressive steps: First, love one's own parents; second, love other members of the family; and not until then you should love members of other families, whether known or unknown.

孝治章第八

子曰：昔者明王以孝治天下也，不敢遗小国之臣，而况于公、侯、伯、子、男乎？故得万国之欢心，以事其先王。

治国者，不敢侮于鳏寡，而况于士民乎？故得百姓之欢心，以事其先君。

治家者，不敢失于臣妾，而况于妻子乎？故得人之欢心，以事其亲。

夫然，故生则亲安之，祭则鬼享之，是以天下和平，灾害不生，祸乱不作。故明王之以孝治天下也如此。

《诗》云：“有觉德行，四国顺之。”

白话译文

孔子说：过去明智的君王依靠孝来治理天下，对小国来的使臣都不敢怠慢，更何况公、侯、伯、子、男？正因为如此，

CHAPTER VIII

GOVERNMENT WITH FILIAL PIETY

Confucius said, "The wise king of the past governed his kingdom with filial piety, and dared not show indifference to the subjects of small states, let alone his dukes, marquises, earls, viscounts, and barons. That's why he won the trust of a great number of states, and came to help make offerings to the wise kings prior to him."

"The ministers who governed the feudal states dared not humiliate widowers and widows, let alone the petty officers and the common people. Therefore, they won the favour of the common people, who were ready to make offerings to the deceased rulers prior to them."

"Those who managed the fiefs dared not be rude to their servants, male and female, let alone their wives and children. Therefore, they won the favour of them all, who were willing to take care of their ministers' parents."

"In that case, it would enable their parents to live a peaceful life when alive, and to enjoy the sacrifices of their offspring when dead. As a result, the kingdom would be in peace and harmony, without natural disasters and contrived crimes. Therefore, wise kings would govern their kingdoms with filial

才得到其他很多诸侯国的欢心，愿意侍奉君王的先祖。

治理国家的人不敢怠慢鳏夫、寡妇，更何况士和平民百姓呢？因此而获得百姓的欢心，愿意侍奉他故去的君王。

治理家庭的人不敢怠慢家臣和女佣，更何况自己的妻子和儿女呢？因此而得家人的欢心，愿意侍奉他的父母。

这样的话，所以双亲在生前能安乐、祥和地生活，就是去世后，也能得到后代亲人的祭奠。因此，天下也就太平无事了，没有灾害，没有祸乱。圣明的君王也是这样用孝治天下的。

《诗经》里说："有伟大的道德品行的天子啊，四方之国无不归顺于你啊！"

piety as aforesaid."

The Book of Songs says, "With such noble virtue, the kings will enjoy the submissiveness of all the other states."

Translator's Notes

1. This chapter focuses on the application of filial piety to the government of a country. The success of the sovereign's government of a country had much to do with his filial piety. If the king treated the people in the same way he treated his own parents, it was not difficult for him to govern the country and to rule the people. There would be no disasters or riots, and the whole world would listen to him and live in peace.

圣治章第九

曾子曰：敢问圣人之德，无以加于孝乎？

子曰：天地之性，人为贵。人之行，莫大于孝。孝莫大于严父，严父莫大于配天，则周公其人也。

昔者，周公郊祀后稷以配天，宗祀文王于明堂，以配上帝。是以四海之内，各以其职来助祭。夫圣人之德，又何以加于孝乎？

故亲生之膝下，以养父母日严。圣人因严以教敬，因亲以教爱。圣人之教，不肃而成，其政不严而治，其所因者本也。

父子之道，天性也，君臣之义也。父母生之，续莫大焉；君亲临之，厚莫重焉。

故不爱其亲而爱他人者，谓之悖德；不敬其亲而敬他人者，谓之悖礼。以顺则逆，民无则焉。不在于善，而皆在于凶德，虽得之，君子不贵也。

CHAPTER IX

GOVERNANCE BY THE SAGES

Zeng Zi said, "May I venture to ask if there is anything more important than filial piety among the virtues of the sages?"

Confucius said, "Of all the things on earth, human beings are the noblest. There is nothing more important than filial piety. Of different aspects of filial piety, the most important is to respect one's own father; and with regard to respecting one's own father, the most important is to pay respects to one's paternal ancestors while making offerings to Heaven. The Duke of the State of Zhou was such a person."

"In the olden times, when the Duke of the State of Zhou was holding the sacrificial rite for the Heaven in the suburbs, he offered a sacrifice to Hou Ji, his ancestor, as well. But when later he held another sacrificial rite for the Five Deities in the Bright Hall, he also offered a sacrifice to Emperor Wen of Zhou Dynasty, his late father. Therefore, people from all the states came to help the memorial ceremony. Of all the virtues of the sages, which could be more important than filial piety?"

"As love generates upon the parents' knee, respect for the parents grows with every passing day. The sages taught others to be respectful, based on the child's respect for its parents, and

君子则不然，言思可道，行思可乐，德义可尊，作事可法，容止可观，进退可度，以临其民。是以其民畏而爱之，则而象之，故能成其德教，而行其政令。

《诗》云：“淑人君子，其仪不忒。”

白话译文

曾子说：我冒昧地问一下（先生），圣人的崇高德行没有比孝道更重要的了吗？

孔子回答道：天地间的万物，人是最高贵的。人的行为没有比孝更重要的。孝行没有比尊崇父亲更重要的。尊崇父亲没有比祭天时将祖先配祀上天更重要的了。周公就是这样的一个人。

以前，周公制定郊祀礼仪时规定在祭祀天帝时附带祭祀始祖后稷，在明堂聚族祭祀五帝时，以其父文王配享。所以天下的诸侯都很尽职，带着贡品从四面八方前来助祭。圣人的德行，哪里还有比孝更重要的呢？

因此，儿女对父母的亲情是孩提时代逐渐养成的，长大后奉养父母也使他们日益尊崇父母。圣人就是依据子女对父母敬重的天性，教导人们要孝敬自己的父母；又依据子女对父母亲爱的亲情，教导人们要亲爱自己的父母。圣人的教化不必严苛也能成功，他们的政令不必严厉，也能统治，根据就是孝道这

taught others to be caring, based on the child's love for its parents. In spite of his indulgent moralisation, the sage succeeded; and in spite of his lenient administration, the sage governed. The ultimate reason for his successful governance resided in filial piety."

"The kinship between father and son is a natural instinct, but it also shows the moral principles between the king and his subjects. Parents give birth to and bring up children, and continue the family tree, of which nothing is more important. In the home the father is king to the child, and at the same time, bonded with love and affection. There is nothing more important than this."

"If the child loves others rather than his own parents, he is said to be anti-moralistic; if he respects others rather than his own parents, he is said to be anti-ritual. If the sovereign wants to educate or govern the people with the offences of morality and ritual, the result will be just the opposite, as the people will have no principles to observe. If the sovereign does not abide by the principle of doing good but indulges in doing evil, he may reach his goal, but the man of virtue will show contempt to him."

The man of virtue behaves differently. What he says deserves the praise of the common people; what he does pleases the common people; his morality and virtue merit the reverence of the common people; his manner of doing things merits the imitation of the common people; his appearance and behaviour are appropriate to the established practice; and his promotions and demotions conform with the rituals. If such a

个根本哪。

父亲与儿子之间的情感，是人类的天生的本性，而君臣关系中与父子关系中的道理也是相通的。父母生养儿女，最重要的就是传宗接代；父亲对子女犹如君王在家，施恩于子女，没有比这种爱心更厚重的了。

因此，不爱自己的父母而爱他人的父母，就叫作违背道德；不敬重自己的父母而敬重他人的父母，就叫作违背礼仪。用这些东西（悖德、悖礼）来顺天下人心、治理人民的话，就把一切都弄颠倒了，因为人民无从效法。不是在身行爱敬的善道上下功夫，相反凭借违背道德、违背礼法的恶道施为，虽然能一时得志，也是君子所鄙视不齿的。

君子则不是这样的，言谈要考虑能得到人民的颂扬，行为要考虑令人民高兴，德义要考虑得到人民的尊敬，制定政令要考虑能够让人民效法，容貌行止要考虑符合规矩，动静进退要符合法度。君子用这样的方式来治理国家、统治人民，因此，人民对君子既有敬畏之心，也有敬爱之情，而且把他作为楷模，模仿他。正因为如此，君子能够成就其道德教化，顺利地推行其政令。

《诗经》里说：“善人君子，仪表堂堂。”

man of virtue governs the common people, they will hold him in awe and in affection, or even take him as a model to follow. As a result, he is able to satisfy the purpose of educating the common people with virtue and morality, and smoothly gives effect to his administration.

The Book of Songs says, "A good person and a man of virtue will have no blunders in his conducts."

Translator's Notes

1. Although the title of the chapter is "Governance by the Sages", it is a further illustration of what was said in the previous chapter, that is, governance with filial piety, because of all the virtues of human beings, there was nothing greater than filial piety. In fact, the sage's way of governing the country and the people is to resort to filial piety. The idea is reinforced by the example of the Duke of the State of Zhou.
2. Why is filial piety greater than any other virtue that human beings have? The answer is: The birth of a child is the favour that the parents bestow the child, so filial piety is innate and is nurtured at an early age, and it grows with every passing day spent together with his or her parents. It is only natural that the child loves and respects his or her parents. It is rather absurd for a child to love parents of other people instead of his or her own. Such a person should not become a sovereign, otherwise the country or the people will suffer. On the contrary, a sage behaves differently, so his governance of the country and the people is to be welcomed and supported by the people.

纪孝行章第十

子曰：孝子之事亲也，居则致其敬，养则致其乐，病则致其忧，丧则致其哀，祭则致其严。五者备矣，然后能事亲。

事亲者，居上不骄，为下不乱，在丑不争。居上而骄则亡，为下而乱则刑，在丑而争则兵。三者不除，虽日用三牲之养，犹为不孝也。

白话译文

孔子说：孝子侍奉父母，平时居家时，要尽量敬重他们；在饮食起居方面，要高高兴兴地照顾他们；父母生病时，要带着担忧悉心照顾；父母去世，要怀着哀悼之心料理丧事；祭祀先父先母（及先祖）时，要庄重严肃，不可随便。这五个方面都做到了，那才算尽到了做子女的责任。

能够侍奉父母的，身居高位而不骄傲自满，身为臣下而不

CHAPTER X

AN ACCOUNT OF PRACTISING FILIAL PIETY

Confucius said, "A dutiful son, when waiting on his parents, should show his ultimate respect for them in daily life; when serving them food, he should make them pleased; when his parents are in poor health, he should take care of them with sincere anxiety; at his parents' funerals, he should be truly mournful; and when making offerings at the memorial ceremony, he should be grave and reverent. When these five are observed, he can be deemed a dutiful son."

"When attending to parents, the son should not appear pompous or conceited, despite his high place; he should not be riotous or rebellious, despite his lower position; he should not manoeuvre against others, despite his low social status. If he is pompous and conceited due to his high place, he is certain to be ruined; if he is riotous and rebellious due to his lower position, he is certain to be punished; if he manoeuvres against others due to his low social status, he is certain to be killed. Without the elimination of these three evil practices, he cannot be a dutiful son, even though he supplies his parents with pork, beef and mutton for three meals a day."

作乱，地位卑微而不和同行争斗。身居高位而骄傲，就会灭亡，身为臣下而作乱，就会遭受刑罚，地位卑微而与同行争斗，就会互相残杀。这三种东西不祛除，即使天天用牛羊猪（肉）奉养父母，仍然是对父母的大不孝。

Translator's Notes

1. This chapter tells what filial deeds are, that is, the concrete things that a filial son should do when he is practising filial duty. There are five things that a dutiful son should strictly observe: respecting his parents in daily life; making his parents happy by supporting them financially; showing anxiety for his parents' illnesses; mourning for his parents' deaths; and being grave and solemn at his parents' funerals. If he has done these things appropriately, he can be said to be filial and dutiful.
2. Besides, there are three things that a filial son should never do: be pompous due to his high position; be riotous due to his lower social status; and tussle with others due his humble poverty. Without the elimination of these three evil deeds, a person cannot be said to be filial or dutiful, even if he provides his parents with pork, beef and mutton three times a day!

五刑章第十一

子曰：五刑之属三千，而罪莫大于不孝。要君者无上，非圣人者无法，非孝者无亲。此大乱之道也。

白话译文

孔子说：有三千种罪可以使用五刑，而最严重的罪行莫过于不孝。要挟君王的就是目无君王，责难圣人的人就是目无法纪，不孝之人就是目无父母，这是天下大乱的根源。

CHAPTER XI

THE FIVE PUNISHMENTS

Confucius said, "There are 3,000 crimes that deserve the execution of five punishments; however, the capital crime is doubtlessly impiety. To coerce the king is to show defiance to him; to calumniate the sages is to oppose the law; to be impious to one's own parents is to show disrespect to them. These are the roots of all serious disasters."

Translator's Notes

1. The five punishments: the first is *mo*, that is, to tattoo the face; the second is *yi*, that is, to cut off the nose; the third is *fei*, that is, to cut off the feet; the fourth is *gong*, that is, to castrate or remove the testicles of a man or the ovary of a woman; and the fifth is *dapi*, that is, to decapitate, or the death penalty.
2. The five punishments in this chapter actually means five categories of punishments, which cover 3,000 crimes of different types. There are a great many crimes, but no crime is more evil than to be impious to one's parents. Impiety is not just evil in itself, it also gives rise to other crimes, or even riots. This is an interpretation of the importance of being pious from a different perspective, and people should be clearly aware of the harmfulness of impiety.

广要道章第十二

子曰：教民亲爱，莫善于孝。教民礼顺，莫善于悌。移风易俗，莫善于乐。安上治民，莫善于礼。

礼者，敬而已矣。故敬其父，则子悦；敬其兄，则弟悦；敬其君，则臣悦；敬一人而千万人悦。所敬者寡而悦者众。此之谓要道也。

白话译文

孔子说：教育人民相亲相爱，最好的办法是奉行孝道。教育人民遵礼顺从，最好的办法是尊敬兄长。改变风气，最好的办法是倡导音乐。要使君王安心，民众顺从，最好的办法是遵循礼教。

所谓礼，也就是敬重而已。因此，敬重他人的父亲，他的儿子就高兴；尊敬他人的兄长，他的弟弟就高兴；敬重他人的君王，他的臣民就高兴。虽说敬重的只是一个人，却能使众多的人高兴，这就是最重要的道了。

CHAPTER XII

THE ELUCIDATION OF THE MOST IMPORTANT PRINCIPLE

Confucius said, "There is no better way to educate the people about loving each other, than to ask them to practise filial piety; to educate the people to be polite and obedient, than to ask them to be respectful to their brothers; there is no better way to bring about a change in morals and moves, than to edify and cultivate them into taking up music; there is no better way to make the kingdom peaceful and the people submissive, than to ask them to observe the rites."

"To observe the rites simply means to be respectful. Therefore, the sovereign's respect for others' fathers makes the sons pleased; the sovereign's respect for others' elder brothers makes the younger brothers pleased; the sovereign's respect for other's rulers makes the subjects pleased. Respect for one person will make thousands and thousands of people pleased. The number of people the sovereign respects is small, but the number of people who are pleased is large. That is the ultimate importance of filial piety."

Translator's Notes

1. This chapter is a further elucidation of the most important principle mentioned in the first chapter. First of all, the chapter shows that this principle includes four aspects: filial piety to parents, respect for elder brothers, music education and the rites. Then it goes on to give the reasons why these four aspects are important.
2. These aspects of filial piety to parents, respect for elder brothers, music education and the rites are fundamental concepts in Confucianism, and everybody should pay attention to them so as to make themselves successful in the society.

广至德章第十三

子曰：君子之教以孝也，非家至而日见之也。教以孝，所以敬天下之为人父者也；教以悌，所以敬天下之为人兄者也；教以臣，所以敬天下之为人君者也。

《诗》云："恺悌君子，民之父母。"非至德，其孰能顺民如此其大者乎？

白话译文

孔子说：君子教人孝道，并不需要挨家挨户去说教，也不必每天当面去教导。（君子）教人孝道，为的是敬重天下所有的父亲；（君子）教人悌道，为的是尊敬天下所有的兄长；（君子）教人为臣之道，为的是敬重天下的君主。

《诗经》里说："和乐平易的君子，是天下人民的父母。"没有至高无上的道德，他（君子）又怎么有如此大的能耐使人民顺从归化？

CHAPTER XIII

THE ELUCIDATION OF THE GREATEST VIRTUE

Confucius said, "When the man of virtue teaches the people to be filial to their parents, he need not go to every household or meet the people every day to elucidate. The aim of him teaching the people to be filial to their parents is to let all the fathers in the world be respected; the aim of him teaching the younger brothers to be respectful to their elder brothers is to let all the elder brothers in the world be respected; the aim of him teaching the subjects to be loyal to their kings is to let all the kings in the world be respected."

The Book of Songs says, "A man of virtue who is joyful and easy-going is the parent of the people." But for such supreme virtue, how could he win the heart of the people and achieve so much?"

Translator's Notes

1. This chapter is a further elucidation of the greatest virtue mentioned in the first chapter. The best way of the man of virtue to make people filial to their parents, respectful to their elder brothers, and respectful to their kings is to do it himself. If the man of virtue could do this, there would be no need to "teach" them by visiting all the households or by meeting all the people. But nobody, without the greatest virtue, was able to do this.

广扬名章第十四

子曰：君子之事亲孝，故忠可移于君；事兄悌，故顺可移于长；居家理，故治可移于官。是以行成于内，而名立于后世矣。

白话译文

孔子说：君子在家尽孝道侍奉双亲，迁移到侍奉君王，必定能忠诚。（君子在家）恪守悌道，尊敬兄长，转移到侍奉官长，必定能顺从。（君子在家）成功处理家政，移到做官，必定能处理好公务。君子在家养成了美好品德，到外面也会有好的名声，因此，这种好名声必然能够流芳于后世。

CHAPTER XIV
LEAVING A GOOD NAME TO POSTERITY

Confucius said, "The man of virtue attends to his parents with filial piety, so he can change his filial piety to his parents into loyalty for the sovereign; he treats his elder brothers with respect, so he can turn his respect for his elder brothers into the reverence for his seniors; at home, he manages his household well, so he can turn his household management into administration of the kingdom. Therefore, the good name of the person, who can be filial to his parents, respectful to his elder brothers, and who can manage his household well, will be left to posterity."

Translator's Notes

1. "Leaving a good name to posterity" was already mentioned in the first chapter, and in this chapter, it is further interpreted, focusing on the relationship between being filial and leaving a good name to later generations. According to Confucianism, the logic is: someone who is filial to his parents and respectful to his elder brothers will be loyal to his sovereign and post, and he, who can manage his household well, can be a good official, because he has the basic qualities of being an official, and will leave a good name to posterity.

谏争章第十五

曾子曰：若夫慈爱恭敬、安亲扬名，则闻命矣。敢问子从父之令，可谓孝乎？

子曰：是何言与，是何言与？昔者，天子有争臣七人，虽无道，不失天下；诸侯有争臣五人，虽无道，不失其国；大夫有争臣三人，虽无道，不失其家；士有争友，则身不离于令名；父有争子，则身不陷于不义。故当不义，则子不可以不争于父，臣不可以不争于君。故当不义则争之，从父之令，又焉得为孝乎？

白话译文

曾子说：像慈爱、恭敬、安亲、扬名这些行孝的道理，已经听过先生的教诲了，我再冒昧地问一下，做儿子的一定要听从父亲的命令，这样才算孝吗？

孔子答道：这算什么话呀？这算什么话呀？从前，天子有七个敢于直言相谏的诤臣，即使天子是个无道的昏君，他也不

CHAPTER XV
FRANK PERSUASION AND REMONSTRANCE

Zeng Zi said, "I have already heard about your teachings of loving parents, respecting parents, maintaining parents, and becoming distinguished and remembered by later generations. May I venture to ask again whether it is filial piety or not when I obey whatever my father says?"

Confucius said, "What did you say? What did you say! In the past, the Sons of Heaven had seven frank admonishers or ministers, who gave forthright admonitions, so they did not lose their countries even though they might have been rather fatuous and self-indulgent; the feudal princes had five frank admonishers, so they did not lose their states even though they might have been rather fatuous and self-indulgent; the ministers and senior officials had three frank admonishers, so they did not lose their families, even though they might have been rather fatuous and self-indulgent; the petty officers had some frank admonishers, so they did not lose their reputation; fathers had frank admonishing sons, so they might not become recreant. When confronted with something recreant, it would not do for the son to keep silent in front of his father, and it

会丧失天下；诸侯有五个诤臣，即使他是个无道的君王，也不会失去国家；卿大夫也有三位诤臣，即使他是个无道的人，也不会丢失自己的家园；做小官的人，能有知己好友直言相劝，就不会做出有损于他名声的事；做父亲的有敢于直言的儿子，也不会使自己陷于不义的困境。因此，父亲做了不义之事，儿子就不可以不向父亲直言相劝；君王做了不义之事，臣子也不可以不直言相谏。因此，当父亲做了不义之事，儿子就一定要直言相劝，一味遵从父亲的命令，又怎么能算孝呢？

would not do for the subjects to keep silent in front of the kings. Therefore, in face of recreancy, the son should admonish his father. If the son always obeys his father, how could he be filial at all?"

Translator's Notes

1. In this chapter, "frank persuasion and remonstrance" is illustrated. To show filial obedience to his parents does not mean that he has to listen to whatever his parents ask him to do without discrimination, for that is not filial piety. The true filial piety is that a son should listen to his parents when what they say is right and appropriate, but that he should not listen to his parents when what they say is not right or inappropriate. Instead, the son should make efforts to persuade his parents to change their minds or to correct their mistakes.

感应章第十六

子曰：昔者，明王事父孝，故事天明；事母孝，故事地察；长幼顺，故上下治；天地明察，神明彰矣。

故虽天子，必有尊也，言有父也；必有先也，言有兄也。宗庙致敬，不忘亲也；修身慎行，恐辱先也。宗庙致敬，鬼神著矣，孝悌之至，通于神明，光于四海，无所不通。

《诗》云："自西自东，自南自北，无思不服。"

白话译文

孔子说：以前，圣明的君王用孝侍奉父亲，因此，祭祀天帝时，天帝能够明了孝子的孝敬之心。（圣明的君王）用孝侍奉母亲，因此，祭祀地神时，地神能够明了孝子的爱敬之心。长幼关系理顺，就可以融洽相处，相安无事。天地之神能够明察孝子的孝行，天地之神就会显灵。

CHAPTER XVI

INTERACTION BETWEEN GODS AND MANKIND

Confucius said, "In the past, the wise king was very filial to his father, so at the sacrificial ceremony of the Heaven, the God of Heaven was aware of his filial respect; he was also very filial to his mother, so the Goddess of Earth was aware of his sincere piety; he was good at dealing with the relationship between the elder and the younger, so he was able to get on well with people of different levels. The God of Heaven and the Goddess of Earth perceived his filial piety and filial deeds, experienced his sincerity, and blessed him."

"Although he was the Son of Heaven, there was somebody who merited his respect, and that was his father; there were people who were born before he was, and those were his elder brothers. He went to the ancestral temple for sacrificial purposes so as to show his lasting memories of his deceased parents and grandparents; he cultivated his moral character and nourished his nature, and acted with caution and discretion, so as not to make his ancestors ashamed of his own blunders. He went to the ancestral temple for sacrificial purposes, and the God of Heaven and the Goddess of Earth would come out to enjoy it. When his filial piety to his parents and his re-

因此，虽身为天子，也有他必须尊敬的人，就是他父亲；也有比他先来到人世的，就是他兄长。宗庙祭祀时，表达对亲人（先祖）的崇敬之意，说明没有忘记自己的亲人。（天子也要）勤于修养身心，行为小心谨慎，担心（不这样做）会玷污老祖宗。天子在宗庙祭祀，以表达对先祖的崇敬之心，先祖的魂灵会显身，前来享用祭品。天子行孝至善至美，与神灵相通，四海之内充满孝的光辉，没有地方到不了的。

《诗经》上说："无论东南西北，四面八方的人没有不归顺的。"

spect for his elder brothers reached a culmination, he was able to communicate with the God or Goddess, whose brilliance would permeate the whole world, and people from all parts of the globe would experience the interaction."

The Book of Songs says, "From west to east, from north to south, there would be nobody who did not want to obey the Son of Heaven."

Translator's Notes

1. This chapter deals with the relationship between Gods and mankind. The power of filial piety is so strong that even Heaven and Earth will feel their filial piety, which will move the Gods, who will, in turn, bless human beings, and the whole world will be in peace and in harmony.
2. Whether you are a sovereign or a member of the common people, you should be filial, because there are always people who are either senior to you or who were born before you. So filial piety is the duty of each and every person in spite of his or her social status.

事君章第十七

子曰：君子之事上也，进思尽忠，退思补过，将顺其美，匡救其恶，故上下能相亲也。

《诗》云："心乎爱矣，遐不谓矣。中心藏之，何日忘之？"

白话译文

孔子说：君子侍奉君王，在朝廷为官时，要考虑如何对君王尽自己的忠诚（甚至可以放弃性命）。退官回家后，帮助推进君王正确的政令，纠正补救君王的错误过失。正因为如此，君王和臣下的关系密切，同心同德。

《诗经》里说："心里爱着他，为什么总不说出来？爱藏在心里，没有哪一天会忘怀！"

CHAPTER XVII

SERVING THE KING

Confucius said, "With regard to serving the king, the man of virtue should consider how to be loyal when he is on the post, and he should consider how to compensate for blunders the king had committed when he resigns and returns home. He should seek to promote the virtue of the king, and correct the king's blunders. Only in that way can the relationship between the king and his subjects be close and intimate."

The Book of Songs says, "We love him from the bottom of our heart, but why don't you let him know? The love that lies deep in our heart can never be forgotten, no matter when!"

Translator's Notes

1. This chapter focuses on the appropriate conduct of a filial person in and out of the imperial court. It is not enough for an official to be loyal and obedient, he should also try hard to help the sovereign, who will sometimes commit errors. The loyal official should make efforts to find the sovereign's mistakes and errors, and stop them, if he is unable to correct them. Only in this way, can it be said that the ruling and the ruled are united in one heart and one mind.

丧亲章第十八

子曰：孝子之丧亲也，哭不偯，礼无容，言不文，服美不安，闻乐不乐，食旨不甘，此哀戚之情也。三日而食，教民无以死伤生，毁不灭性，此圣人之政也。丧不过三年，示民有终也。

为之棺椁、衣衾而举之，陈其簠簋而哀戚之，擗踊哭泣，哀以送之，卜其宅兆而安措之，为之宗庙以鬼享之，春秋祭祀以时思之。

生事爱敬，死事哀戚，生民之本尽矣，死生之义备矣，孝子之事亲终矣。

白话译文

孔子说：孝子的父母去世了，会哭得声嘶力竭、上气不接下气；不会像平时那样在乎仪容仪态；说话时不会讲究辞藻。穿漂亮的衣服感到不安，所以不穿；听悦耳的音乐不感到愉悦，所以不听；吃美味的食物不感到好吃，所以不吃。这是父母亡

CHAPTER XVIII

MOURNING FOR DECEASED PARENT

Confucius said, "When his parent passes away, the dutiful son should be unaffected in lamenting, receive guests without paying attention to appearance, speak without careful wording, feel too uneasy to wear fine clothes, too sad to listen to music, and lose appetite for any delicious food. They are all the results of mournful sadness. However, three days after the parent's passing away, the son should break the fast, and begin to eat. The dutiful son should be instructed not to harm his own health due to his parent's decease, and should not endanger his own life though he was too sorrowful to pay attention to his appearance. That is the assertion of the sage. The time for mourning should not be longer than three years, which makes the people aware that there should be an end to everything."

"The inner coffin and the outer coffin should be prepared for the deceased parent, who was then laid on quilts and shrouded in cerements, together with plates of sacrificial offerings. The living should beat the breast and stamp the feet to show deep sorrow, and prepare a decent burial. A cemetery plot should be chosen for the deceased, and a family temple should be constructed for the living to hold memorial

故后子女应有的悲戚之情。父母去世的头三天，孝子不能进食，但三天后必须进食。不要因为父母去世伤了自己的身体，这也是不孝的表现。即使悲伤影响了身体，也绝对不能危及性命，这是圣人的教诲。为父母服丧，最多不过三年，圣人要大家明白，不管什么事，都有结束的时候。

为死者准备棺椁，穿好寿衣，盖上被子，抬入棺内。摆上盛有食物的簠簋等祭品，以寄托生者的悲痛和哀伤。(出殡时,)要捶胸顿足，嚎啕大哭，悲伤地送葬。占卜墓地陵园，安葬灵柩。建造宗庙，使亡灵有所归依并享用生者的祭祀。每年春秋两季举行祭祀仪式，以表示生者对死者经常的缅怀。

父母在世时，孝子用爱和敬侍奉他们，父母去世后，则怀着悲恸的心情料理丧事。这样，生者就是尽到了根本的责任，即孝道，从父母生前的奉养，到父母死后的安葬祭祀，孝子该做的事全都做完了，到这时候，孝子事亲的任务就结束了。

ceremonies. Every season the living should go to the temple to pay their regular respects to the deceased with rich sacrificial offerings."

"When their parents are living, the dutiful sons treat them with love and respect, and when they are deceased, the sons make arrangements for a decent funeral with grief and sorrow. By now, the dutiful sons have shown their perfect filial piety before and after their parents' deaths. And that is the end of their filial piety."

Translator's Notes

1. This is the last chapter of *The Book of Filial Piety*, and elaborates on filial piety concerning parents' deaths and funerals and sacrifices, which might be said to be the last things a filial son should do for his parents. When his parents are alive, the filial son should treat them with proper rites, and when his parents pass away, the filial son should do all the things according to proper rites as well, including the ways of mourning, the arrangement of the funerals, and the ways of sacrifice. By now, the filial son has brought these responsibilities for his parents to a successful close.

图书在版编目（CIP）数据

三字经 千字文 孝经：汉英对照 /（宋）王应麟，（南北朝）周兴嗣著；孟凡君，彭发胜，顾丹柯注译. —北京：中译出版社，2015. 11

ISBN 978-7-5001-4230-0

I. ①三… II. ①王… ②周… ③孟… ④彭… ⑤顾… III. ①汉语－古代－启蒙读物－汉、英 ②家庭道德－中国－古代－汉、英 IV. ① H194.1 ② B823.1

中国版本图书馆 CIP 数据核字（2015）第 181325 号

出版发行 / 中译出版社
地　　址 / 北京市西城区车公庄大街甲4号物华大厦六层
电　　话 / (010) 68359376，68359827（发行部） 68359719（编辑部）
邮　　编 / 100044
传　　真 / (010) 68357870
电子邮箱 / book@ctph.com.cn
网　　址 / http://www.ctph.com.cn

出版策划 / 张高里　刘香玲
责任编辑 / 刘香玲　顾　恬
封面设计 / 廖　铁

排　　版 / 竹叶图文
印　　刷 / 深圳佳信达印务有限公司
经　　销 / 新华书店北京发行所

规　　格 / 960mm×640mm　1/16
印　　张 / 20.25
版　　次 / 2016年2月第一版
印　　次 / 2016年2月第一次

ISBN 978-7-5001-4230-0　**定价：**69.00元